Talking Poetry

Talking Poetry

Conversations with Ashok Vajpeyi

RAMIN JAHANBEGLOO

OXFORD
UNIVERSITY PRESS

OXFORD
UNIVERSITY PRESS

Great Clarendon Street, Oxford, ox2 6dp,
United Kingdom

Oxford University Press is a department of the University of Oxford.
It furthers the University's objective of excellence in research, scholarship,
and education by publishing worldwide. Oxford is a registered trade mark of
Oxford University Press in the UK and in certain other countries

First Edition published in 2022

Impression: 1

Published in the United States of America by Oxford University Press
198 Madison Avenue, New York, NY 10016, United States of America

British Library Cataloguing in Publication Data

Data available

Library of Congress Control Number: 2022943850

ISBN 978-0-19-286918-0

DOI: 10.1093/oso/9780192869180.001.0001

Printed in India by
Rakmo Press Pvt. Ltd.

Contents

PART IV: THE PASSION FOR MUSIC

PART V: A PLURAL INDIANNESS

Introduction

The Magus of the East

'All thought begins with a poem', said the French philosopher Alain. As such, the difference between a poet and ordinary beings is that a poet thinks closely to the world. A poet lives with poetry, since to live without poetry is not to live. This is a *mysterium tremendum* (as Nietzsche calls it) which is lost by our contemporary decivilizing society. Only poets can give us the possibility to transcend the basic inhumanity at the heart of our civilization. The last hundred years remind us of what Paul Valery said in his essay *Crisis of Mind*: 'We civilizations now know that we are mortal'. However, poets come to our lives unexpectedly and 'create a new alphabet of hope' as affirms Ashok Vajpeyi.

Poetry is always a miracle necessary for the survival of language. Every poet opens a window onto a new world. Because as George Steiner says: 'The death of language is the death of the universe of possibilities.' We need poets to tell us what are these possibilities. As Ashok Vajpeyi says: 'We don't go to poetry to search for or reach the truth, but to experience reality, to be part of it. Poetry does not proclaim the truth or research it: it sculpts its fiction from reality. Every poem is a narrative of an incomplete reality'. This is the difference between poets and ideologues. Poets have the integrity of thought and a fundamental honesty not to declare reality complete. 'After the end, we won't be finished', writes Ashok Vajpeyi. There will always be the incomprehensible and the incompleteness.

Being a poet is a fragile condition in our world. In the Middle Ages, poets could seek refuge in monasteries to escape the barbarians and defend the language. Where can poets seek refuge today to keep the words safe? They need to wrestle with reality to write in its margins. These margins are a living dialogue with what Paul Celan calls 'north of the future'. What gives a poet his/her dignity is the force of silence. Perhaps a

Talking Poetry. Ramin Jahanbegloo, Oxford University Press. © Ramin Jahanbegloo 2022.
DOI: 10.1093/oso/9780192869180.003.0001

poet knows how to live silently. To be silent is to think closely to one-self. None ever succeeded better than poets. Let us consider the silence which inspires Ashok Vajpeyi in few lines of his poem entitled 'Ancestral homes': 'Calling the saddened gods in vain—in an infinite cosmic journey—we will go to our ancestral homes'. This *at-homeness* is what Heidegger calls 'dwelling' after the German poet Holderlin. Heidegger and Holderlin see the essence of the 'poetic' by way of its relation to this dwelling. As Holderlin affirms: 'Humans dwell on this earth, Full of Merit, but also poetically.' Dwelling in this world is equally dwelling in language. The more the poet dwells, the more he/she becomes the one who thinks. The poet speaks and thinks as he/she dwells. Now, the poet who speaks and thinks defends the word, because as Stefan George underlines: 'Where word breaks off no thing may be.'

Ashok Vajpeyi is a poet who is at home with the word. He speaks to the mortals and the divinities. He makes the mystery of the world visible to us by speaking with/of poetry. 'Words dwell in silence and, are at peace there.' As Heidegger says: 'Poetry is the act of founding by word ... that which endures.' That is why poetry is closer to us than any other form of writing. Poetry endures like the world does. Therefore, poets are in no hurry with words; readers are. When a poet writes poetry, he/she grows in it. Poetry needs a time for ploughing and a time for gathering the har-vest. We often forget, just how much the poet is close to the grammar of the earth. It takes a poet like Ashok Vajpeyi to remind us: 'Being earth, nonbeing sky.'

The point I have been trying to clarify is simple: poetry is organically bonded to the essence of language. A poem is charged with the promise of the ontological echo of words, which sometimes is set against the word itself. Shakespeare's *Richard II* is in this sense magical:

> For no thought is contented: the better sort,
> As thoughts of things divine, are intermixed
> With scruples, and do set the word itself
> Against the word.

Throughout these conversations we encounter a poet who sets his own pace through poetry, music, and painting. Ashok Vajpeyi's deep sense of expectation from arts is born out of his love of the world, which renders moral dignity to creativity. But perhaps, this is because, he is in search of lines of Pasternak and Akhmatova, Kabir and Ghalib, Bonnefoy and Char, in a poetic haven, where he can 'lament only in poetry, because there's no other space left for regrets or dreams'.

Ramin Jahanbegloo
New Delhi, March 2020

PART I
FROM DURG TO ST. STEPHENS

1

Childhood Memories

RAMIN JAHANBEGLOO (RJ): You were born on 16 January 1941 in the city of Durg, which was then in the central provinces and is now in Madhya Pradesh.

ASHOK VAJPEYI (AV): Now, it is in Chhattisgarh. I have no memories. I was only born there because those days there was a normal convention that a married daughter for her first child would go to her parents'. My mother had gone to her parents, my grandparents. My maternal grandfather was posted in Durg, he was a civil servant. So that is how I was born there. But I don't remember anything because I was perhaps there for a few months. Then I shifted to Sagar which actually became my home town. Many years later when I knew that I was born in Durg, I went to look for the place and there was a possible old British bungalow in which my grandfather used to live. So that is where I must have been born. In a poem that I wrote later I tried to re-arrange facts of my life as 'permitted by poetry but not by history'. There was a bit of a play between them to say if I were to change what I would do: I would still like my mother to go to her parents for my birth, but instead of being born in a town I want to be born in a village where my grandfather could have gone on a tour and my mother, with some obstinate insistence, would have accompanied him. There would have been some theatricality in that, being born in a town there isn't much.

RJ: Yes, well these are the contingencies of being history and being born in different places. But, you mentioned the name Sagar, how long did you live there?

AV: In fact I lived there almost for 19 years, until I graduated. All my schooling and graduation took place there. Sagar was a small town; it had a cantonment and a military encampment during the Second World War. There was a place called Macronia where they had army barracks and it was said that Hitler had on his map Macronia marked,

Talking Poetry. Ramin Jahanbegloo, Oxford University Press. © Ramin Jahanbegloo 2022.
DOI: 10.1093/oso/9780192869180.003.0002

as a possible place to be attacked, if he ever attacked India. It was a very big military set-up there. And my university, from where I graduated was located there where I was a student till 1960, in these barracks, of the old British army. My father was a University official and my grandfather in whose bungalow, some years ago, I was born, had retired, and he was living in a house opposite ours I used to be going across, most of the time. I, in fact, lived more with my grandfather than my father.

RJ: That was at what age?

AV: It must have been from the age of one. My initial schooling took place in a kasbah khurai in Sagar District, where again my grandfather was posted. My father was then moving around here and there because the University had not yet come up. But from the third standard in the primary school I came over to Sagar and I lived there till I graduated.

RJ: We will talk about your schooling, but before the independence, that is until the age of six you used to see a lot of British soldiers around?

AV: Well I would not know because they did not come to the town as much. But I do remember seeing some British officials. I mean there were very few cars in the city. We had a civil surgeon who had a car so he would move around and that was quite a rare sight because on our road in my *mohalla* to have a car coming was a bit of an event.

RJ: There were only bicycles or ...

AV: Bicycles and Tongas, nothing else. The other thing was I never studied in what are known as the private though strangely called public schools. I studied in a primary school which was a municipal primary school and my further school education. I joined a government school which was not far from where we lived.

RJ: How did that happen?

AV: Because after having finished my primary school I had to go to a high school. And there was Swedish mission and other schools in the city but my father chose the government school. And in those days the government institutions had some prestige, it is something they lost over the years. At that point of time it was supposed to be one of the best schools in the region and I must say I was very grateful to that school because it is there that I found my lifetime mentor/teacher one Lakshmidhar Acharya, he came in the 9th standard. Only two years he was there. But he was an incredible teacher, he never came to class with a book. He just came like that and would ask, 'What subject today?'. He used to teach History, English, Hindi, Sanskrit, Arabic, Persian, Urdu, Marathi, Gujrati, all these subjects.

RJ: So he was a homeroom teacher actually, we call it a homeroom teacher, I mean teaching many disciplines at the same time.

AV: Well yes it was common those days.

RJ: So you spent 8 hours with him?

AV: I became his pet student. We became guru and disciple and he was there only for two years but almost every evening I spent with him walking, talking. With him I had my very first cup of tea, because tea was forbidden in our household, for children. We were given only milk, no tea.

RJ: Why?

AV: Because tea was thought to be poisonous, not good for health for children. I never ate out because this was again sacrilegious. I ate out in a restaurant, a samosa for the first time with him. I saw my first film with him, I heard my first classical music concert with him, I can't even recall now how many things I did with him for the first time.

2

Discovering Poetry

RJ: You broke a lot of taboos?

AV: Yes taboos, small ones. After two years when he was transferred, we the students were all very unhappy, sentimental and wailing, and all that. He put his hands on my shoulders and said, 'my dear boy you come from a family of administrators so you should get into the Indian Administrative Service, but die as a poet'. Now at the age of 14–15 you don't think of death, and here was my teacher telling me to die as a poet. Anyway, he initiated me into contemporary writing in Hindi, classical music, and much else.

RJ: When did he pass away?

AV: He passed away much later; I think in the 80s.

RJ: But you kept in contact with him all the time?

AV: No, I could not. He moved away. For some time there was contact but then I lost it. But by the time he left I had already started writing poetry and the interesting thing was that I never wrote on children's page, I never revealed my identity as a student. Thinking that if they knew that this was a poem by an 8th or 9th class student, they would throw it away. I started getting published. And by the age of 16 which is when I passed out of the school, I had already published in many prestigious journals of Hindi. They were immature perhaps stupid poems I think, as I look in retrospect. But that time in a small town, someone was trying to do something new, must have persuaded or impressed the editors who published them. So it was that kind of … the world in Sagar until the school days … I started public speaking … taking part in school debates and I seemed to have developed some kind of a gift of the gab, I used to win most of the competitions in public speaking. Whenever there was an inter-school debate contest or something like that, they would say if he was coming we aspired for the second or the third place because he would take away the first.

Talking Poetry. Ramin Jahanbegloo, Oxford University Press. © Ramin Jahanbegloo 2022.
DOI: 10.1093/oso/9780192869180.003.0003

Anyway, all this because my teacher also gave me instructions on that. He told me that you should make fun of yourself right in the beginning so that the audience would give you license to make fun of everybody else. If you can't say something in 10 minutes you won't be able to say it in 100 minutes either. Say serious things with a laughing face, you don't have to pull a long face to say something serious. And fourth one was don't pour a bucket full, just give a glass of it. Leave them thirsty, hungry, whatever. These things stayed stuck in my mind.

RJ: Do you remember the first poem you wrote?

AV: Yes, I remember the first poem in January 1950 (RJ: at the age of nine), when I was in the 6th standard and India was becoming a democratic republic on 26 January. All kinds of celebrations were planned in schools and I wrote my first poem, in praise of the new republic.

RJ: Patriotic poem!

AV: It was a poem hailing the new republic and ... I did not fully understand what the damn republic would mean. But I wrote in its praise enthusiastically. It was some kind of a quatrain. From then onwards I started writing poems. Even prose-poems under the impact of Tagore's prose translations of Geetanjali. Also, some things in metrical verse. By the time I was 16, I came under the impact of the movement of the new in Hindi and I gave up metrical verses and started writing free verse.

RJ: At what age did you start reading poetry:

AV: Quite early. I think as early as when I was 10 or 11 years old. I started looking for poetry books.

RJ: Under the influence of your mentor?

AV: No, the mentor was not there at that time. Just out of curiosity, I started imagining myself to be a poet. There were local poets, poets whom I would listen to and attend their readings and things of that kind, so it was an initiation, maybe at the age of 12/13.

RJ: So why poetry and not prose?

AV: This choice never occurred to me; poetry almost came naturally. Prose I thought was more tedious. In fact I wrote a bit of prose when I became the editor of our school magazine. The school magazine used to come out in manuscript. When I took over I decided to print it. So the first-ever issue of the magazine in print came out. I wanted all kinds of things to be there, including a play, a short story, and some other essays. There were not enough fellow students writing that kind of material. So I wrote myself under different pseudonyms. I wrote an autobiographical account, I wrote a play. I wrote a lot of prose later, largely critical. I had even started writing an autobiography, quite stupidly, at the age of 15 when I had hardly anything by way of life to write about. I wrote a few pages thinking that it could be one mode of prose with some storytelling.

RJ: Did you show your poems to your father and mother?

AV: No! I was quite afraid of my father. My father was a kind of an authoritarian person. He had been connected to writers when studying in BHU and Allahabad University. He belonged to Uttar Pradesh. My father came from a farmer's rural family but he had studied in Banaras Hindu University and Allahabad; did his M.A. in Economics. Actually two things happened under his influence—I became very secretive about my poetry as that was not something people usually approve; they thought it was some nonsense. I was a reasonably talented student, used to come first in my class, used to get distinction in every subject I took. That created a kind of a defence for also being a poet. My being a poet was tolerated. It was seen as a hobby that would fade away sooner and later. The other thing was that I started discovering some younger poets, aspirants to poetry there were in town. One of them became my close friend. We became a duo, we would walk together, read together, etc. His name was Ramesh Dutt Dubey. He died a few years ago. He remained all his life in the town. Another interesting thing happened in 1957. When I was about to be 17 years old, a major literary conference of Hindi writers was being organized in Allahabad. And Allahabad in those days was the Mecca of Hindi literature. There were two places Banaras and Allahabad, which mattered and made or marred literary reputations. I got invited to this conference. It was surprising as I had very little to show only some poems that were published in important journals. That created a bit of an uproar in the University campus because we had a very eminent and senior Hindi critic as the head of the department of Hindi. He was my father's cousin but he was, we thought at that time, very anti new trends and we were a group of persons trying to follow this new trend in our town and our university. We were not looked upon kindly by him. He got invited and, of all persons, I got invited, and none of his colleagues, juniors and disciples! He got so enraged that he did not go. And I went. It was my first kind of literary journey and I met a large number of major as well as young writers of my language, a very thrilling experience.

RJ: So did you ever read non-Indian poets at the time?

AV: I started reading them more seriously when I went to the University. Initially I was a science student. I was rather good in physics, mathematics, and chemistry, and I did academically well in all these subjects in the first year in the university I studied science and I topped in the University.

RJ: Where was that, what University?

AV: Sagar (RJ: Sagar University). But then I thought, I should not be planning to get into being an engineer or a doctor or something professional like that; I would rather be an academic or perhaps an administrator. So the humanities suited me better. I shifted. And it was during that period, I started equipping myself, and starting to discover the whole wide world of literature and poetry. Luckily we had a very good library in the University. I read Rilke, Eliot, Yeats, a whole lot of them. Even Pablo Neruda, Nazim Hikmat, all in English translation.

3

The Nehruvian Ideal

RJ: Was your English at a good level?

AV: Well, I would say reasonably good though my entire education till graduation was in Hindi medium, English was only a subject, but that did not prevent one from acquiring a reasonable level in English I still believe if you are rooted firmly in your mother tongue you can acquire command over any other language quickly. But if you are not rooted in your mother tongue, apart from losing your legacy, cultural and otherwise, you can't do the same thing so easily. In fact I did not take Hindi in school as a subject, 9th standard onwards, for three years I studied Sanskrit instead of Hindi. And for my B.A. also Sanskrit, English Literature, and History. In order to assert our independence from the orthodoxy of the Hindi department we started two things—one, some of us younger writers got together and we started a journal in Hindi. Only two issues came out, the first one in 1958 the second one in 1959 and then it died because we never had the financial resources to sustain it. However, almost all the significant Hindi writers of that time contributed in these two issues. They cooperated because they must have felt moved by the fact that a young group of unknown persons in Sagar was trying to do something new and thereby participating in the ongoing struggle to establish the new in Hindi. We also created a forum, called *Rachana*. All its invitations were issued in English, using some French words as well, only to tease the Hindi department! But we had at least two very important Hindi writers Agyeya and Muktibodh come and speak under its auspices. A lady teacher from the faculty of the English department presented a paper on the Russian theatre theoretician Stanislawski. My father was a University official and I topped in the Bachelor of Arts examination. Sagar University was a big university, it had nearly 100 affiliated colleges all over Madhya Pradesh. My father said, everybody

Talking Poetry. Ramin Jahanbegloo, Oxford University Press. © Ramin Jahanbegloo 2022.
DOI: 10.1093/oso/9780192869180.003.0004

thought, I did so well here because he was in the administration, I had better get out and prove myself elsewhere. He wanted to send me to Allahabad; he, in fact, got me admitted there. But I, by that time, had thought that Allahabad as a literary centre was receding and many important Hindi writers had shifted to Delhi, so I should go to Delhi. In 1960 I came to Delhi and got admitted in St. Stephen's College for my M.A. in English literature. I was there for two years, Aspiration to appear in the civil service examinations was there so I wanted to take up a teaching assignment which would not tax me too much. I got appointed in Dayal Singh college and I taught there for two years. Later I appeared in the civil service exam and qualified for both the Indian Foreign Service (IFS) and Indian Administrative Service (IAS). I decided not to take IFS, because I wanted to keep on living in my mother tongue, in its invigorating geography and ethos. In fact at one level I did not want to go into administrative service either because by that time I started feeling that teaching was much more engaging and satisfying. I was teaching English Literature. Shakespeare, Galsworthy, etc. It was enjoyable and I started wondering why should I go into rather a dull profession of administration! When I told my father on the phone that I had qualified, and thereby proved I could do it, but I didn't want to get into it. Because I would be thrown away from a life of imagination and ideas. He sternly retorted asking me if I could recall the conversation in the staff room of my college. I was stumped and failed to recall anything significant. I said they kept on talking about promotions, dearness allowances, and whatever, but nothing intellectual. My father then asserted that if I wanted to be in the realm of ideas and imagination I need not be academic. 'Go into the civil service. If after two three years you feel that this is not going to be in keeping with your ambition; leave it. You have a brilliant academic record, and could get a scholarship, to go to Oxford or Cambridge and do a proper PhD and become a proper academic.' I gave up and joined the IAS.

RJ: I want to go back to your family and talk a little bit more about your parents. Were you born in a religious family? I want to go back to try to ... because we jumped very quickly. First of all I want to go back to your family, and talk a little bit more about your father, mother, siblings ... were you born in a religious family?

AV: Well my mother was religious, very religious in fact. But my father was a bit of an agnostic. My mother used to worship *Ram Charitra Manas* which is Tulsi Das's *Ramayana*, a great epic in Hindi. She would open the book where she left the previous day and read the next verses and then put some flowers on the pages by way of worship, rice grains, etc. She used to worship the great book, every day. At the age of nine I read the *Ramcharitmanas* at one go with my grandfather in about nine hours. He was a very religious person. I had a religious family, but somehow I lost faith by the time I was 16 or something. (RJ: Was it poetry that made you lose faith) I don't know, perhaps … There used to be a Bengali sweet shop. Every city in North India then used to have a Bengali sweet shop and Bengali sweets were very delicious and different from the usual north Indian desserts. I and my friend, Ramesh Dutt Dubey, went there. The shop used to open at 4 and close at 6 and would finish everything because the Bengali owner would not make more. We ate in leaf cups. We threw the leaf cups outside, where there was an open running gutter. Once two boys, who were perhaps waiting, jumped at them, got hold of them and drank the sweet juice left. That made me feel very bad. I said to myself what kind of a world this was. For two years I stopped eating sweets. I gave up sweets and I think I also gave up God. Much later I got married and a lot of Hindu rituals were observed. When I came back home with my wife we were made to go and worship a Peepal tree, a well, apart from offering flowers in a Hindu temple. It was a traditional way of expressing gratitude and seeking blessings from all that surround your daily life and sustain it. So this empathy, somehow, I retained. The idea is that we are grateful to the world and its elements—water, fire, earth, sky, air. This gratitude found way in my poetry. It is deeply ingrained in me. My mother never insisted that I should observe any rituals. Neither did my father who was an agnostic. He carried out some of the basic religious rituals during marriages, Holi, Diwali festivities, poojas, etc. I never thought that he was fully in it. On the other hand, my grandfather and grandmother, who lived right opposite, used to be very religious. So was my mother. Later I wrote a poem in which I seemed to have felt that my gods died much before I was born. Ours was in any case a liberal religious family.

I was the eldest of eight children of my parents. We were four brothers and four sisters, a large family, out of which I think all my brothers are, more or less, non-religious though perhaps spiritual. But my sisters, at least two of them, became deeply religious, the other two I have my doubts. But any kind of demonstrative excessive religiosity has always been out of the question in our family. There was no such thing. I **remember** two events from my boyhood. One was the assassination of Gandhi. I was seven years old when the news came. There was a complete lull set on our *mohalla* and no food was cooked in any family. There was one shop which made some puris and sabzi to be distributed to us children. There was no cooking in our house nor in any other house. Also on the 13th day, each house in the mohalla observed the 13th day, which is a Hindu sort of celebration after the death, and I was very struck. Later I wrote a piece 'A Death in Every Family'; it appeared as if a death had taken place in every family, which was incredible and yet very moving. There was only one radio in the entire mohalla and we heard the running commentary on the last journey of the Mahatma on it. There were two commentaries—one in English and the other in Hindi, and sometimes the commentators' voices would start choking with emotion, while they were speaking. The adults and children alike would start weeping sitting in that room where the radio set was kept. There were about 200 people outside. None of them could hear anything, since during those days the radio sets were rather elementary and they used to make gargling sounds and one could not hear clearly for long. There would be a wave of weeping that would go out, and those 200 odd people, who had heard nothing, would also start weeping or sobbing!

RJ: This reminds me of the Shi'ite processions with a weeping crowd.

AV: Yes and that left a very deep impact on me (RJ: Were your parents involved in the independence movement?) No, my maternal grandfather was in that he had, as a magistrate, released the freedom fighters on bail and, therefore, was by way of punishment, demoted. One of my grand uncles was part of a semi-revolutionary anti-British outfit. I would say that, only being born a few years before independence, we were largely products of freedom, rather than struggle for freedom.

RJ: So after independence, the Nehruvian ideal.

AV: Yes of course the Nehruvian ideal. Around 1958 Nehru came to Sagar, to lay foundation of the Library of the University. There was huge excitement. All roads of our town were improved and we all lined up on them to see, greet, and cheer him up. But before that in 1950, sometime in early January the first President designate of India came to Sagar to deliver the convocation address at the university. Interestingly he was staying in the circuit house which was close to our house. My father was a University official and he was assigned the duty of looking after Dr Rajendra Prasad. The day the convocation was to take place, my father was going to the circuit house, he took me along. Just a young nine-year-old boy, I could not have gone to the Convocation to look at the first President of India. We went and in the room he was staying he was not there. We started looking for him. He was sitting in the garden. We approached him to find that he was mending with a thread and needle, one of the buttons of his jacket. The man who in another fortnight or so was to take over as first President of India was sewing a button! That also left a deep mark on me. I developed deep respect and fascination for both the Nehruvian elegance and the Gandhian simplicity.

RJ: How was your home lifelike, with eight children, you were eight no?

AV: My uncle, the elder brother of my father, had died, and his two daughters were also brought up with us, we all grew up together. In fact we were 10 (RJ: So a lot of noise in the family!?) Yes, so I used to withdraw to my grandfather's house. And there on the upper floor there was a room, where I would study. Then there were my aunts, my mother's younger sisters who were studying in the university. It was a very crowded family, where everyone would look into the others' doings but somehow we also could find moments of solitude, I then started having this, kind of a dialectics, if you like, of trying to seek solitude inside home but seeking company outside with friends, conversations, and arguments, etc.

RJ: Did you have a close relationship with your siblings?

AV: Well since I was the eldest and was thought to be talented and remarkable in their eyes. So there was a bit of a distance, and this distance grew with age. At the age of 19 I left Sagar and my family and came over to Delhi. Thereafter there was no going back to Sagar, even though my parents lived there till much later. I would go for a short while. As civil servant I started getting posted to several places.

RJ: Did you play with other children?

AV: Yes, in fact I created a cricket club and we used to play cricket. There used to be a Company Garden right behind our house. The British had created these gardens everywhere, and we used to play there. We got somehow convinced that Gandhi was murdered by the RSS. There used to be an RSS *shaakha* nearby taking place, and one of the teachers who used to live close to our place used to conduct it. We would go and disrupt by throwing, stones on it rather un-Gandhian! Out of sheer spite, because we were convinced that they had done it. That remained in my mind forever.

RJ: So are you the same—same anti-RSS

AV: Yes very strong anti-RSS, and I seriously consider that RSS is a smaller threat to Islam and a bigger one to Hinduism because it is a very distorted parochial version of Hinduism, narrow, hatred ridden quite unlike what it largely never was and what it never should be.

RJ: I read a year ago in the papers that they suggested to make a temple in the name of Godse.

AV: Yes, but it was a move by the Hindu Mahasabha. They are a part of the same mentality, fanatics. I do think that RSS out of power or RSS in power, it does not lose any of its fanaticism.

4

Poetry against Fanaticism

RJ: So you think poetry cannot go on with fanaticism, anywhere.

AV: Yes, anywhere … all over the world. Poetry could be all kinds but never fanatic. It could be verse but not poetry; I believe that fanaticism or extremism or absoluteness, claims to absolute truth by anybody, religion, science, or whoever is unacceptable in poetry. Poetry believes in relative and human truths and cannot possibly posit that there are absolute truths to be propounded or discovered or asserted.

RJ: So you can write poetry in physical ghettos but not in mental ghettos.

AV: Yes, you can use poetry as resistance. So in a ghetto you are using it as resistance, but in a mental ghetto poetry is not possible. Perhaps, sadly, prose is.

RJ: I wanted to ask you, this feeling of Indianness. When did you get it? Were you proud of being an Indian?

AV: Frankly I have never been proud of being an Indian. I think it is an unnecessary pride. We can barely feel proud of being human, given the fact how we keep on acting, in so many inhuman ways! I only feel Indian when abroad, when you are meeting people from a different civilization. Then you start feeling, that you are somewhat different. To go back a bit, my father was very close to the family of a Muslim professor of geography. So much so that when one of my sisters was getting married we waited before the seven customary rounds were completed, for the Muslim couple to come and watch it. Then there was a communal riot in 1963 in Sagar. I was not there, but I was later told that my father had seven Muslims take refuge in our house with a view to protect them, from the Hindu fanatics. One of them, a neighbour was wanting to attack them, but had great respect for my father. He came and said that he knew that my father had kept these Muslims inside his house. My father admitted but also asserted that he had a gun and anybody who tried to touch them would be shot by him. All

Talking Poetry. Ramin Jahanbegloo, Oxford University Press. © Ramin Jahanbegloo 2022.
DOI: 10.1093/oso/9780192869180.003.0005

this contributed to my understanding of otherness. I think in poetry there are no others. In life there are many others, but for most of them you should be grateful. But for them you could not have done many things, whether they are others in terms of your menials, your opponents, your intellectual rivals, your creative adversaries. All these are others and they all in one way or another make your life worthwhile. Religious others, caste others, I have never accepted this kind of otherness all my life.

RJ: So the lesson of tolerance and humanism you got it from your father mainly, no?

AV: Yes and from my mother as well. I think I am very much a creation of literature. I mean if literature could be credited or burdened with creation of some kinds of human beings I would think that I am created by literature. And in literature, this dichotomy between us and them gets demolished. Literature makes you realize that 'they' are 'us' and 'we' are 'them'. Look at Milton who wrote this amazing poem 'Paradise Lost' and he declared right in the beginning that he was writing it to 'justify ways of God to Man' but he ended up justifying ways of Satan to God. And Satan is more powerful than God in the poem! Surely there is no doubt about the deep Christian faith of Milton, but Christian faith and the poetics can take two different directions. In a way the other supersedes the intention or belief.

RJ: When one writes poetry or prose, he or she is free. This is the difference with being fundamentally a religious person.

AV: Yes, creativity could be constricted by such restrictions or exclusiveness. Therefore the idea of othering people is completely unacceptable to me. In our case these days there is othering of a vast number of people in India. They are not a few, they are millions and you can't do that except by damaging critically your creativity and imagination, your conscience and humanity.

RJ: You said that you are a creation of literature. Do you remember, which books at a tender age influenced you the most? When I was a kid of 10, I read a lot of novels.

AV: In my case I would say that my earliest influences came from Hindi literature, from people like Tulsi Das who incidentally has been notoriously interpreted as a Hindu poet in a narrow sense, which I don't think he was. Anyway, and then later, when I became a little more inquisitive. I read Rilke, Rilke is a big influence on me, and others such as Yeats and Eliot. Then novels of Tolstoy, Dostoevsky, they opened an entirely new world that where again it was difficult to find simple enemies or binaries.

RJ: How can one portray you as a young man reading Tolstoy and Dostoevsky?

AV: I mean both, losing religious faith but picking up some elements of spirituality and secondly discovering faith in the world. I was not moved by ideas that make you drift away. I was caught in deep love and lure of the world. I cannot wish away the world, how can you ever! Insufferable, in many ways, economically, politically in many ways the world is becoming insufferable. But I cannot give it away. It is this world that we have to grapple with, we have to deal with, we have to change if we can, dream alternatives of, but without the world we cannot be. I can go to a Himalayan cave or wherever it is, whether in mind or in geography. No, I don't want to run away and yet I am not under any obligation of any sort to accept the ugliness, the atrocities, the cruelty of the world.

RJ: So you always wanted to confront the ugliness and atrocities of the world with your poetry?

AV: Yes to the extent one can. There are limits to your confrontation and to your talent; there are limits to your imagination. But I would like to think that the whole idea that the world is worth celebrating, the world being worthy of being enchanted with is an idea that got ingrained in my mind through literature. Religion got replaced by literature if you like. There is more plurality possible in literature than in religion, also more empathy.

RJ: At what age did you discover the three concepts of 'evil', 'love', and 'beauty'?

AV: I would say I discovered beauty quite early, in the sense we had beautiful trees and birds (RJ: In an empirical way?) yes empirically and the other kind, love, in fact I fell in love with my cousin which was sacrilegious (RJ: at what age?). At the age of 16. It did not last for too long and it never amounted to anything, but it was furious on both sides. It was, of course, highly unacceptable to my mother (RJ: Why?) Because in a Hindu family, a cousin is a cousin, she is your sister, and you can't fall in love with her. Then I fell in love at the age of 19 with a fellow student, and that was while I was at University and we were classmates. This was happily full-blooded love with deep passion. These years were, in a manner of speaking, innocent; so they were songs of innocence, no concept of evil at that time. I could not imagine how atrocious and how violent human beings could be.

5

How to Be a Civil Servant?

RJ: But you were talking about Gandhi's assassination.

AV: Yes, there was that but it was not enough to conceptualize it. I think I became aware of evil through the novels of Dostoevsky. By that time, I had also gone through Mahabharatha and Ramayana and they had very evil characters. So some notions started building up. But I would say that it was a period where innocence dominated over all else. But evil, eventually, evil in the world came up (RJ: You wrote on Auschwitz). I became aware of the evil not so much physically, not in my world so much until I entered bureaucracy. And bureaucracy in India does not exist merely in the State, it exists all over the place, in the Universities, for instance, which are conceptually autonomous. But all autonomous institutions are invariably bureaucratic as well. They follow the same hierarchical structures and rigidities. I discovered that there was something evil in the State itself. The State cannot sustain itself without resorting to some aspects of evil, like hegemony, conspiracy, domination (RJ: This is what Tolstoy believed in). Yes, all these lessons that I had found in novels and learnt in literature, I had found them imaginatively but not experienced them direct in my life, until I entered bureaucracy. And there I found that there could be, there was inexplicable evil. There was no cause, there was no explanation, there were no reasons which created evil. So evil is in some sense, and this is a very disturbing thought, evil is autonomous. It does not need a cause. In most cases, I mean evil of ideology, evil of state ... all these kinds of manifestations, sites of evil.

RJ: But from 1965 onwards, you were the cultural secretary of Madhya Pradesh.

AV: Yes, because I increasingly realized the real nature of the State. There were two kinds of possibilities, one possibility was that you become a part of this huge gigantic irreplaceable uncontrollable apparatus of

Talking Poetry. Ramin Jahanbegloo, Oxford University Press. © Ramin Jahanbegloo 2022.
DOI: 10.1093/oso/9780192869180.003.0006

evil, the other was you take a marginal role and branch off into something, where the evil would not disappear but where you need not face it in the same manner or measure. That is why I chose culture and education. These were not areas where evil was so dominant like in commerce or industry and such other sectors. So I became sort of a marginal civil servant, a specialist in marginality!

RJ: And you got involved in politics.

AV: Well, later, during my civil service I kept away. But the fact that I was close to some and not so close to others, did involve me in some kind of politics. But they were elected persons and I had to work with all kinds, I had no choice (RJ: But you were close to Mr Singh, that was what involved you in politics). Yes, but I did not get involved in his politics. Arjun Singh was a very cultured politician, he had great regard and concern for culture, a Nehruvian creature. He did not understand modern art, he did not appreciate classical music personally but he understood that these were important and had to be promoted. He allowed me to do what I wanted to, because he trusted me. Secondly, we shared the essential liberal ideals. As long as he was at the helm of the affairs he did not allow anybody to interfere in culture which I was looking after. The state did not interfere either. It was a very unique model in Madhya Pradesh where the state was creating a vast infrastructure of culture, but the state was not interfering, was allowing experts to do what they think was proper and was trying to resist and prevent any political or ideological interference.

RJ: I would like you to say a few words about *Bharat Bhawan* because this is an institution that you created yourself.

AV: In 1980 Arjun Singh became the chief minister of Madhya Pradesh for the first time. Before that we had talked about an independent department of culture. In the state governments in those days, culture often existed as a part of education department and, therefore, it never received any proper attention or resources. I used to argue that culture was an important area and it should not become just an adjunct of a larger department. And Arjun Singh appreciated this. So within three months of his taking over as CM he created an independent department of culture and I was made the first Secretary of Culture. And, very unusual for a civil servant, I remained Secretary of Culture of

Madhya Pradesh for 10 years. Those were the 10 years in which we endeavoured to change the cultural ethos of Madhya Pradesh.

RJ: What was so special about Madhya Pradesh?

AV: Unlike UP and Bihar it was not so caste-ridden. It had elements of it but not on a big and restrictive scale. It had seven neighbouring states, which no other state had at that time. And Chhattisgarh was also a part of MP as long as I was there. So you had Bihar, UP, Gujrat, Rajasthan, Maharashtra, Andhra Pradesh, and Orissa. The seven states on the borders, each one of them contributed. There was a kind of cosmopolitanism and MP was emerging as a kind of a protestant arm if you like of the Hindi Church. Frankly when I returned to MP after teaching for a couple of years in a Delhi college and then a year of training in the National Academy of Administration in Mussoorie I had no idea of its cosmopolitanism, its openness. It came upon me later when I started doing my work in culture in MP. I spent nearly 26 years in MP as a civil servant. I had to leave MP for good in mid-1992. There was more openness, more support for innovativeness. We had Kumar Gandharva who originally belonged to Karnataka, but came to MP for cellubial climate. He created a new kind of music within the classical mode. We had Gajanan Madhava Muktibodh—a major poet who created an entirely different kind of poetry and a relentless interrogative poetics. We had Sayed Haidar Raza, whose house you are sitting in, who created an alternative indocentric modernism all the way in France. All this was possible because they were all from MP and they had the ethos where this kind of innovative, courageous departures could be generated and sustained (RJ: So kind of a Vienna of India). Yes, perhaps a little immodestly I must admit that at that time we became Vienna. Bhopal, before was a city of 3 B's Burquas, Beebies, and Buffaloes, with very, thin creative culture, other than the culture of cuisine and shikaar, and a bit of Urdu poetry.

RJ: So that is why you left Delhi after St. Stephens and went to MP?

AV: I would never have left MP until the BJP came to power. And they started interfering. The problem with the BJP is two-fold. One that they have an ideological stance that makes them feel and claim that they understand culture (which of course they don't), and they interfere in the name of culture. All ideologically inspired outfits, whether communist, or RSS, they have an interfering vision. I had a running battle with the leftists though I agreed with many of the ideas of equality, of justice, against exploitation. But I could not agree with the idea of regimentation … which they somehow cannot avoid nor accept plurality.

RJ: But later, they made a harsh critique against you and called you a power broker disguised as a poet.

AV: Well I had gone through all that. It is a strange irony that there were many who at that time were vociferous in condemning me, accusing me of dictatorial tendencies. My dictatorial tendency was only to prevent bureaucracy and politics to interfere with culture. There I was rather dictatorial. But in my work, I created, discovered, and nourished areas of plurality. We invited the leftists and also invited persons who were not leftists—Nirmal Verma, Vidya Niwas Mishra, etc. But the leftist cannot presumably be comfortable in a space which is not dominated by them. They have this tendency, either you are with us or against us. I could not take that position, not only because I was a public servant but also because I was convinced that there were and must be different ways of looking at the world. Perhaps the narrow parochial ways of looking at the world are not really worth bothering about. But there are alternate ways of looking, so I always sought those spaces and none could find fault with that. I went through all that. I fought back. I confronted them in no uncertain terms, but I did not hesitate to accept and invite the talented ones amongst the leftists. Now, as a strange irony, the leftists invite me in their fora. They have come away far from the days when they used to pass resolutions against me, boycotting me, boycotting institutions. But some of the saner individuals even among the Marxists kept on coming to our seminars, readings, festivals, etc. It did not affect our work in any substantial way, but it did create a huge irritation.

RJ: Yes, because now you are a national poet, but in those days they saw you as a civil servant.

AV: This was one ground of attack and nonacceptance. I organized more than 100 poetry festivals and public readings of poetry including Indian, Asian, and World poetry festivals in Bhopal and readings all over MP. But I never featured in them as a poet. I said, no, I was the organizer, I should not figure as a poet I am now working on a biennale of Hindi poetry, but I would not feature in it as a poet. I published a large number of books of poetry and criticism, during that period and none of them were ever reviewed in the journals I was editing or supporting. I did nothing unethical on that count. The record has been clean. Also, mercifully none of them ever accused me of dishonesty. All civil servants end up getting accused of corruption, some kind of money-making and all that.

6

Politics and Poetry

RJ: To end this chapter, I want to go back to politics and poetry. You were never interested in ideologies, but you were attracted by politics. Why did you became a civil servant?

AV: No, I would not say that I was attracted by politics, in the sense that I never thought that political power was central power in our times, I never accepted that position. In my own institutional work, in civil service, I did not allow the political to dominate, I allowed the artistic, to restrict, constrain the political from dominating. My lifetime mission, if any, has been to counterpose the accepted images of power, of the politician, the film actor, the corporate executive, of the criminal, of the player with those of writers, artists intellectuals, etc. This may be politics of a different kind. This is not seeking political support; this is trying to subvert the dominant politics. That's what I feel I did. My interest in politics comes from my abhorrence of ideology. I think ideologies have done great damage to the world. It is not only here in India though here too they continue to do so, they are doing it all over the world. I acknowledge the fact that ideologies have also created great art, great literature, but greatness was attained by those people who were able to exceed the ideological framework. The moment of exceeding could create greatness. But ideologies exist. You cannot wish them away, so you have to grapple with them. So I tried, perhaps not very successfully, to create a situation where literature and arts are also seen as ideology. And they are an ideology that does not seek power. I believe there can be an ideology that does not seek power. It generates ideas and insights, wisdom about human condition, human predicament, human possibility.

RJ: I am sure that you are very conscious about the fact that in the 20th century there have been many examples of poets who were involved with politics. You had examples like You have Saint John Perse and

Talking Poetry. Ramin Jahanbegloo, Oxford University Press. © Ramin Jahanbegloo 2022.
DOI: 10.1093/oso/9780192869180.003.0007

Octavio Paz, who were diplomats. As for Mao Tse Tung, he was a great politician who also wrote poetry. So why poets are interested in politics?

AV: You know Thomas Mann famously said 'in our times human destiny presents itself in terms of politics'. Politics is the most dominant force of our times. This is not only our times, all times since Plato, but, more importantly say from the 19th century. Politics is an important force. You cannot wish it away, you have to address it, you have to find a connection with it, you have to hold a dialogue with it. Whether politics wants to hold such a dialogue with other forms of human endeavour or not is another matter. Perhaps it does not need them. Although there have been times when politics had needed, for its legitimization, for its validity, etc. art and literature, but it may no longer need them. For instance today RSS does not need validation from art and literature, most of whose practitioners are moved by narrow parochial vision. Whatever the language, whatever the style, and whatever the region, this is the problem they are facing: they do not have intellectuals of any stature, they don't have writers, artists of any consequence with them. The only people who are ambivalent are classical musicians and classical dancers. But a bulk of creative community—poets, writers, novelists, critics, painters, sculptors, art curators, etc. are not with them. It is another matter that the creative community is a minority, does not matter. But, there are situations in which minorities matter, specially in a democratic polity.

RJ: This reminds me of what Pablo Neruda said in September 1969 when he wanted to be a candidate for the Chilean presidency. He said that his life was never divided between poetry and politics. Politics came to him naturally, because he wanted to be close to the people. So I have the feeling that though you were never attracted by ideologies like communism or anarchism, politics came to you in a very natural way. I mean you became interested in as a poet because you were be interested in the lives of Indians. Am I right?

AV: In a way you are right. But I never aspired for a political position. There were times when some well-wishers came to me asking me to try to be a member of the Rajya Sabha, I said no, that was not my cup of tea, I never wanted to be a part of active politics. If you like I am a part of a creative intellectual politics without being necessarily drawn to actual politics. There has to be if you like a politics of creativity and imagination, a politics of plurality, a politics of courage and conscience, and I feel that you can practice this politics meaningfully and creatively only by not being in actual politics. That is the irony of the situation. Some writers, artists have been nominated to the Rajya Sabha. But none of them mattered, they made no impact in the Rajya Sabha. They lost a lot of goodwill outside by being nominated. The issue quite simply is that you can say there is a politics, but that politics is more intellectual, less practical, actual, work-a-day politics. Normal politics these days all too after is bereft of any sense of morality or moral responsibility. But there ought to be an alternative politics, away from power, its distortions, corruption, a politics of conscience and courage. And that is a politics a writer can help evolve and practice. I am acutely aware that such a politics which does not have the dynamics of social action, mobilization and solidarity is doomed. It is doomed to fail. It can hardly influence the real conditions of living. But such failure has certain nobleness, certain moral glow. In a work a day world where success, by hook or crook, is such a dominant element, failure assumes a certain negative glory. I believe poets in our times are beings who invariably fail but make failure significant and enriching, noble and human.

PART II

HOW TO BE AN INDIAN POET TODAY?

7

Living with a Poetic Tradition

RJ: You hold a very unique position among contemporary poets of India. First, because it is impossible not speak of you as a modern poet. Second, because your use of metaphors and images is a sign of your Indian sense of empathy. Would you describe yourself as a typically Indian poet?

AV: Well, I don't know what a 'typical Indian poet' would mean. Firstly, I do not belong to those generations and there are some of them in India, who can be called disinherited generations. That is to say that they have gone into modernism in such a manner that they seem to have lost all memory of their own heritage. I have consciously avoided doing that because I do not think it is possible for a truly Indian poet to disinherit this rich heritage and face the modern dilemmas and modern experiences imaginatively and sensitively. In the Indian tradition there has always been a possibility to change within tradition. It is not like the binary created largely in the West where tradition and change are pitched against each other. In our case the change takes place within tradition. I belong to that trend where my memories, linguistic, racial, metaphors, and images and symbols of the tradition are still very eminently usable to describe, explore, enact whatever may be the so-called modern experience. For me poetry is also a civilizational matter. It is not that you have this personal expression and whatever your pains and joys, your despair, your hopes and anxiety, which are all very good material for poetry, but poetry is also an act of civilization and, therefore, you cannot write as if this civilization doesn't exist or this civilization has merged into some vague amorphous human heritage. I don't believe that. Much as I owe a lot to the West, much as I have learnt from the West, much as the kind of modern that in India has now been

Talking Poetry. Ramin Jahanbegloo, Oxford University Press. © Ramin Jahanbegloo 2022.
DOI: 10.1093/oso/9780192869180.003.0008

dominating, is a literary endeavour propelled by the West, there has been a tradition where out of the restlessness within tradition, a different kind of modernism was already taking place from 13th/14th century. It was partly also a product of perhaps or a consequence of India's encounter with other traditions, Islamic, Arabic, Persian, which came in and they deeply influence Indian creativity, in poetry, in music, in architecture, in visual arts. And there is a restlessness with tradition in Kabir, in Meer and Ghalib, in many others. There was a kind of modernism born out of India itself. It had nothing to do with the West. The more dominant trend of the West propelled modernity come into existence in the late 19th century, early 20th century and it tended to obscure or marginalize the other Indo-centric modernism in that sense. I tend to feel I belong to that rather than to the West propelled modernism.

RJ: A philosopher like Heidegger believed that language is a dwelling of Being. If you accept this view for your poetry, then maybe we can say that there is a cosmopolitan mode of being that makes a poet out of you.

AV: I would say it is a cosmopolitan way of being with very strong rooting in India. I would not pose them as one against the other. For me this being cosmopolitan is not possible without being Indian. So it emanates from there. There is a kind of, shall I say, a critical formulation that creates these binaries and in an actual act of creative imagination they do not exist. In the sense that there are many people who see the Western kind of modernism as the dominant form. They are a prey to it and they are a part of it and yet, subconsciously in their structures, in their patterns of memory, in their choice of metaphors and symbols, they cannot but hark back to their own centuries-long creative articulation in India.

RJ: If I had to use a metaphor I would compare your poetry to a tree which has its roots in the Indian soil but goes up to a worldly sky.

AV: Ah yes but this again is not an unprecedented or unique phenomenon. This has happened in the Indian situation all the time. People came from outside, people brought ideas from outside, it happened during the Indo-Greek period, in sculpture for instance. It happened later with the Mughals and Muslims, it happened with the

West. So I mean everything is absorbed and the stream goes on. It is not a river which is formed by entirely local sources, but also not a river which is formed entirely by waters that flow from outside. So it is a mix. And that mix I think is potent, creatively enriching, and also challenging.

8

Choosing Ancestors in Poetry

RJ: Do you feel close to master poets in the West? Poets like W.H. Auden, Dylan Thomas, T.S. Elliot, Akhmatova Pasternak. Do you feel closer to romantic poets or to spiritual poets?

AV: It is very difficult to choose your true ancestors in poetry. Where do you get from what is difficult to identify? But I must say I was greatly influenced by Eliot and W.B. Yeats in the beginning and I was rather critical of Auden, who according to, my teacher was not able to handle human suffering in a deep way. That was my understanding, maybe I was wrong, but that's what I thought. And then, people like Pasternak, in case of Pasternak—the idea that we are 'envoys of eternity held hostage by time' has been of echoing in my mind for a long while now. The idea that there is eternity and there is time. The idea that there is time and timelessness, which idea incidentally was also in T.S. Eliot. The notion that, for instance, the job of poetry whether by choice or by compulsion is to offer willy nilly, some kind of a resistance. It is resistance to cliché, it is resistance to generalization, it is resistance to totalization, it is a kind of a resistance, and it is a recall to what is seen to be on the margins. There are love, presence, desire. For instance. I have written very erotic poems and the reason I did so was two-fold— One, I thought here was a great Indian tradition of erotics which is comparable only perhaps to the Egyptian tradition of erotics or the Chinese and no other, in the West you did not have that kind of a tradition. And we have lost it to a Victorian mindset which had become dominant in our education, educated middle classes. I thought it is well worth reviving in contemporary terms, this sense of the erotic. It is a sort of a non-sematic, if you like, trend. The other was that in times of massive amnesia created by politics, by markets, by ideologies, by the state, it could only be resisted by memory. And memory cannot be merely individual memory, there is such a thing as civilizational

Talking Poetry. Ramin Jahanbegloo, Oxford University Press. © Ramin Jahanbegloo 2022.
DOI: 10.1093/oso/9780192869180.003.0009

memory. Memory should not be lost, it should be reanimated in some sense in the creative act. In my poetry I have used phrases from Kalidas, Jaydev, Amaru images of the Vedic classical Indian literature, I have used images from Ghalib and others, etc. Because after all why should not I inherit, not only my civilizational heritage, but also the entire human heritage? Then, of course, you make your choices for your own poetic concerns, make your own particular structure. You cannot claim to have inherited everything; whatever you do is by choice. For instance, I have been influenced by the Polish poets, especially Czeslaw Milosz and Zbigniew Herbert. Herbert particularly who, I thought, was a man who was trying to look at the entirely contemporary modes of torture, suffering, and alienation and making us see that they have classical origins and they happen all the time. And then the humility to say that this was not 'an act of courage but a matter of taste'! I thought that the Polish have mastered the poetics of Satyagraha in that one should stick to one's truth whatever may be the consequences. Not stay away from your truth. In their boldness that I found indirect ways of doing it. In the given circumstances Milosz had to leave Poland, but through poetry he lived all his life there. They had to find ways of physical survival. And they deeply touched me and I thought here was something, unique and very inspiring. European poets had occupied our imagination until we discovered the Middle Eastern European poets. Hungarian, Czech, and Polish and such like who were different from the Russian and who had found some freedom to express the realities that they saw and suffered. And there were the Latin American Neruda and Paz who had a very expansive cosmic viewpoint and they somehow resonated better because they had a world view as enacted in poetry, which was similar to the Indian feeling of expansiveness, big lands and everything being a part, whether it was winds or rivers or mountains, all becoming part of you, as it were, your very domestic landscape. So that also resonated. All these experiences from other poets, other traditions had gone into it.

RJ: It seems to me that your quest for truth is very close to the Upanishadic nature of search for supreme reality and the absolute. Do you try in poetry to reveal a relationship between the individual and the absolute?

AV: You know I would say even truth is something which you strive for, seek for, and never actually arrive at. Now, part of the existential despair that is there in my poetry is kind of a product of this phenomenon that you strive for truth or something absolute and you never reach there. The more important thing is the quest, rather than the goal. The more important thing is to try to make that journey rather than arrive somewhere. If you reach the goal the poetic work would be unnecessary. My firm truth is my poetry, not some truth above or beyond it. There is no truth away from poetry which I am trying to approximate through any means. No, for me the process is the truth.

9

Levels of Consciousness

RJ: So for you, your poetry is actually like a journey, let's say like the journey of Odysseus, but is there a return to Ithaca, or there is no return?

AV: Well there is no return, and there is no hope of reaching anywhere. In fact, in some of the later poems specifically I keep questioning myself. What you started for is in reality turning into nightmare! Is this what you had imagined would happen or is this entirely because others have conspired to do it or is it that you are also complicit in it in some ways? This is the kind of ambivalence or anxiety at the core. It is not just disappointment; it is something deeper where you start questioning the journey itself. Perhaps this is a particularly modern stance, if you like, that there is no destination.

RJ: But at the same time there is an evolution in your poetry and I think you are very conscious about it. I would add that in this journey you go through different levels of consciousness.

AV: Yes that is true. I am glad that you have read my poetry carefully.

RJ: How do you see these different levels of consciousness?

AV: I have always believed in plurality. Plurality of structures, plurality of language, and plurality of even consciousness. You cannot possibly operate merely at one consistent continuous consciousness. In any case it would continually get disrupted, subverted, added to by other forms of consciousness. And somehow poetry must be able to resonate this. And, therefore, I have tried in some ways to take one idea and explore it in many ways. For instance I have written a lot many poems about death, of specific persons but also death, absence in general. There was a duet of poems, one says that after death there would be nothing, it would be the final end, which is a very modern belief. On the other hand, there is the other belief that there is another life, that you are born again and that is the other poem. And between

Talking Poetry. Ramin Jahanbegloo, Oxford University Press. © Ramin Jahanbegloo 2022.
DOI: 10.1093/oso/9780192869180.003.0010

the poems I have not taken a position whether this is desirable or this is not desirable, or this is true or this is not true. As a poet it is not for me to judge. I am having both these levels of consciousness.

RJ: Let us take a poem like 'The Tree' In the poem you say 'A tree does not summon anyone, it only organizes the space'. This invokes in my mind a zen garden.

AV: The point is there are all kinds of ideas, images, echoes from here and there. I would not even sometimes know what source they come from because I am not consciously summoning them. There is this idea that objects have life of their own, a tree for that matter or a book, inanimate objects, all of them have life of their own. Things also look at us and it is not as if only we are looking at things. The idea that a poet should have empathy which could also bring this into the poetic structure, that you are being watched not only by other human beings but also being by other objects, other forms of being—maybe a bird or a tree or a stone. This is very much a part of Indian tradition wherein the epics, stones speak, or trees turn into one thing or the other. All kinds of metamorphosis take place. I think this is a widening of human imagination. The Indian imagination to begin with and for a long time was a much wider and richer imagination. It was not homocentric. There was no overriding belief in India that man was the centre of the universe. There was a belief that the world was multicentric and that there are others, things other than humans that have equally made this world and which existed in this world. I think that was a richer and wider imagination; it started shrinking under the impact of the modern which became very homocentric. So in our world some beings exist and other objects are purely instrumental. You use them for this or that—a chair or a pair of shoes or a table and I have written poems on all of them, making them come alive through poetry, to register their live presence. I remember Vasko Popa a Yugoslav poet who had written a series of poems about pebbles. Even Zbigniew Herbert did this—unusual in the European tradition. In European tradition obviously there have been elements that allowed for life in many different forms and objects.

RJ: Therefore, we can speak of the element of non-human and the natural in your poetry.

AV: In fact physically I had never lived very close to nature. Because I was a city lad and there was not much around, except trees and a garden behind my house, The Company Garden. But trees, etc. have always fascinated me, birds, and things of that kind. But I am not a nature lover in the sense that I go to the Himalayas and spend time or go to some natural beauty spot. I have visited them occasionally but basically my physical life has been confined to the more stubbornly human rather than natural. Therefore poetry compensates for the physical loss of nature in day-to-day life in a certain sense. What I cannot do physically I do in poetry, in other words.

10

A Vision of Nature

RJ: Are we dealing here with a linear process of time or with a cyclical time?

AV: It is a cyclical time. Linear process of time does not interest me at all and that is one major difference I perhaps differ from many fellow poets in Indian languages. For them the linear has become the more dominant and the more modern. For me the historical, linear time, I would not say is not central, it is only one kind of time. I do not give it more than that in terms of importance or dominance. I live a physical life in which the linear time dominates, but again in poetry other times are evoked and the poetry seems to compensate the loss of them in actual physical lived life.

RJ: Is it also a way of conquering time?

AV: Well I would not know if it is a way of conquering time but surely it is an attempt to exceed the limits that are imposed upon you by time. Limits on your existence, on your survival, on your imagination, all these are circumscribed by time. In a way you can say I am trying to cut through time to figure out something which could, for the lack of a better word, is timeless. But the problem with that in poetry is that you cannot reach the timeless without going through time. Its only through time that we reach the timeless, not the other way round. It may be some kind of dialectical way of dealing with time. Time has been my obsession anyway.

RJ: Yes, I have seen that in your poetry, but are we dealing here with what we can call the cosmic geometry of the poetic language, is there a cosmic geometry?

AV: I am deliberately or consciously not doing it, but now that you say it, I would say yes, because I seem to. I don't believe that the stars do influence your life and fate or that the moon makes you lunatic! I simply do not believe in all that. But I do believe that there is a connection

Talking Poetry. Ramin Jahanbegloo, Oxford University Press. © Ramin Jahanbegloo 2022.
DOI: 10.1093/oso/9780192869180.003.0011

between all of us. I have a sort of cosmic view, if you like, in believing that we don't only live in our language, we don't only reside in a country or place, we don't only live in this world, we live in cosmos as well. And in the cosmos everything is connected to everything else and that every element in the cosmos is responsible for every other element. And I believe in fact that rivers and forests and trees and birds and animals not only feel responsible for us, they have fulfilled this responsibility much better than homo sapiens. There is already a kind of failure there and I feel sad, and disappointed. I would like to believe that there is a tear, in empathy, in the eyes of a star somewhere when I weep here on earth!

RJ: It is interesting that you mention the concept of empathy because I wanted to ask you if we can eventually say that this cosmic way of living is a combination of aesthetics and ethics?

AV: I do not believe in pure isolated aesthetics, nor do I believe in ethics independent, untouched by, unsoiled by aesthetic touch. For me the two co-exist in a deep relationship.

RJ: Take the example of someone like Brodsky who said aesthetics is the mother of ethics.

AV: But for him because the circumstances in his life were such, the aesthetics became the source of courage, the source of defiance, the source of trying to go beyond the limits. So for him, more importantly, aesthetics gave ground or support for ethical action.

RJ: But for Brodsky, poetry is a form of dissent and such it is an alternative mode of thinking and living. Is it the same for you?

AV: Yes, in fact in the same interrogation, the judge asked him, who had decided that he was a poet and he said 'Who has decided that I am a human being?' So there is this complete identification of poetry, courage, imagination, and stand. A viewpoint which may or may not be congenital or acceptable to powers that be. It is mostly unacceptable to all kinds of power whether democratic or despotic.

RJ: I am trying to understand more about your aesthetics. Does Rasa have a significant place in your poetry?

AV: Well directly, no. You see what has happened is that the way traditionally Rasa used to be understood was to give delight and pleasure through various emotions. Now to give delight and pleasure is not aimed at in my case. I am not writing to delight or I am not writing to give pleasure, they are if at all by-products. My poetry may delight some people, but it is not as if you are planning to do it or that you have aimed your poetry to do it. That is what Rasa theory meant at some point. But for instance, Romans believed that the job of poetry is to delight and instruct. Many poets have been combining aesthetics with ethics. What to do, what not do and yet give you pleasure. Pleasure principle and reality principle were seen largely as irreconcilable binaries. In the Indian tradition pleasure and reality get invariably tied up. You cannot give pleasure unethically by the same logic, in poetry you cannot be ethical without being aesthetic. But for a poet it is enormously problematic. Aesthetics has to be rooted in ethics, or the other way round. And this is not an easy matter though there is no choice, in terms of an either/or choice. In India there has been a long tradition of didactic poetry when you are trying to tell or instruct people, issuing poetic commandments—do this or do that. I do not subscribe to that tradition. It's not the job of the poet to tell you what to do. My job is to create a sense of reality and yet to doubt it. That this is my sense of reality, it might or might not be real because I am looking from a certain point of view and my own viewpoint, my location, my time might be influencing it.

11

A Heraclitean Poet

RJ: When you write poetry do you think about your readers?

AV: Oh no, and this may be true for most poets. I think in my case, in the case of many other poets that I know of, the other is within you. So when you are writing a poem you are actually talking to this other in yourself. There is a conversation going on there and that conversation is addressed to this other and your imagination brings you and the other together in moments of creativity. We are after all complex constructs, it is not as if the other exists only outside, at least for a poet, for a writer. There might be difference between prose and poetry, but I would still assert that you write without keeping audience in mind and you also write without knowing where it is leading to. You see a poem may start with an idea or a word or an image or some other provocation of some kind and you do not know what is going to happen and you might end up in something which you had never anticipated, never expected. So a good poem will always surprise the poet as much as it surprises others. And if it does not surprise you, if it does not delight you by surprise, if it does not make you feel that you have done something worthwhile, you cannot expect that this would do something similar to others. You are your first critic. If you are an alert conscious person and you are not just doing it by way of routine exercise, as you go for a walk you write a poem! A poem could be wonderful and surprising like a dawn but it cannot be a routine morning walk!

RJ: I would like to go to the roots of the word 'critique' which in ancient Greek means to distinguish. Do you can distinguish between the reality and imagination when you are writing poetry?

AV: Well you know for a poet any neat boundary between reality and imagination does not exist. He imagines reality and realizes imagination in some sense. For him it's seamless. You do not know you are now

Talking Poetry. Ramin Jahanbegloo, Oxford University Press. © Ramin Jahanbegloo 2022.
DOI: 10.1093/oso/9780192869180.003.0012

going from reality to imagination or that now you are falling back into reality from imagination. But, for purposes of analysis, it might be necessary to distinguish between the two. I would say that although I hope that my poetry has a strong sense of reality, I think it has a stronger sense of imagination, and for me a poetry without imagination and with only chunks of reality would be an uninteresting enterprise. Poetry is a way of imagining the world. If you are imagining the world you cannot be imagining in a vacuum or a void. So there is reality which impinges upon your imagination. Imagination becomes rooted in that sense.

RJ: This flow from reality to imagination in your poetic language gives me the impression of a Heraclitean movement. For example in your poem 'Not the Same' there is feeling of a clear movement.

AV: Yes, movement really fascinates me. This morning in a seminar where I was giving a valedictory, I was trying to say that India never had the concept of a still life. We had a very important Hindi critic espouse a theory of beauty as *karma saundarya*—that there is beauty in action, there is no beauty in anything static. A still life, perhaps Indians would not find that beautiful. You go to all these sculptures, there is a movement. In Ajanta wall paintings, in miniature paintings you would always discern movement. This movement I think is one of the characteristics of the *homo sapien:* existence constantly on the move, sometimes involuntarily. Many times we are being dislocated, migrating against one's own wishes. But there is this movement and I think movement is important. At least for me it has been important so it attracts my attention. Although stillness and silence also attract my attention; it is not that I overlook them but movement is the more cardinal. It also gives you opportunity to discover new images of a certain kind or moments in those images which may go unnoticed if it were frozen into some permanent stillness or some unmoving stillness.

RJ: Does the movement of the world make you fearful or does it make you humble?

AV: Sometimes fearful, mostly humble. But sometimes surely fearful, in the sense that sometimes when I see these huge architectural constructions, whether the Pyramids or Taj Mahal or these kinds of things they make me fearful because they are so solidly there, almost perfect.

On the other hand you go to the Jama Masjid here, you go to a temple, Khajuraho, wherever there is a movement, they are fixed but there is movement around them which also creates beauty. I remember an incident, in Krakow there was Milosz centenary festival and there was a church, Corpus Christi where Szymborska, I, and two other poets were to read. We were told that this was the richest church in Poland, it had so much gold. Although you were not supposed to speak, and only read your poems, at the end of my reading I said thank you very much, I have never read my poetry surrounded by so much gold in my life! I know poetry is an unholy act and thank you for inviting me to read in a holy place! Because in India the distance between poetry, literature, and the temples and masques for that matter, is quite large almost unbridgeable. Temples are not used for poetry readings and things of that kind. Though in the West in spite of the so-called secularization, they have concerts in churches, poetry readings take place in churches, which is quite remarkable.

RJ: Actually, art, spirituality, and philosophy are very close.

AV: Yes in fact the kind of spirituality that exists in literature and art is the spirituality which is again informed by a large cosmic consciousness. It is born out of what I call love and lure of the world but sees beyond it. And, therefore, it has similarities with other versions of spirituality. Luckily I think the arts and literature do not call for a belief in god or any ritualistic forms of expression. It is a non-religious spirituality which is not bound by faith. It is another kind of spirituality. And, sadly, there is little recognition that poetry, literature, the arts are also equally valid forms of spirituality like religion or some other so-called holy forms. But whether there is recognition or not, this is the reality. And, specifically, in India where the spiritual has been almost usurped by the most unspiritual forces! The spiritual has been used in a very uncivilized, crude, grotesque manner. It's more important, because then the spiritual becomes radical. It becomes an act of resistance. A lot of atrocities take place in India in the name of religion, community, caste, etc. All this violence in a manner of speaking invalidates the claim of these forms, whether of religion or politics, invalidates any spirituality they might have owed allegiance to. I firmly believe that poetry and the arts are perhaps the last ramparts of spirituality.

That if the spiritual also disappears from them, then the world would have been disastrously, outrageously, irretrievably desacralized, de-spiritualized, even emptied, evacuated of any meaning or purpose. It would be a very great human loss. It is loss of imagination, it is loss of creativity, it is loss of empathy and interconnectivity, it will shove you into a void, a vacuum where the divorce between aesthetics and ethics would be complete and final.

RJ: Would say that we need poetry to bear life's tragic burden?

AV: Well poetry has helped in this through ages. It has to help you bear the burden and it has to assert in any case the fullness, the richness the human possibility of all life. I mean it has to make one feel that alternatives are possible, that there are different ways of looking at the world, that the world can still be saved and whatever may happen we can still be human. So poetry in a manner of speaking operates in a simultaneity, operates in a sphere which more visibly belongs to politics, that is the sphere in which possibilities are being concretely talked about, aspirations are being articulated. But distinct from these possibilities, poetry creates the other possibility, the possibility of dreaming, of imagining, of empathizing, of questioning, but also of celebration and adoration. All these are also brought by it in the realm of the possible.

RJ: Also, maybe the possibility of recovering the meaning and the intrinsic value of the world? Wouldn't you say that?

AV: Yes. You know the world has been another of my obsession. Language itself is one of my major obsessions if you like, my major concern. And I attribute to 'word' a certain indestructibility. Somebody said that you have no belief in god but you have a deep belief in word! I think in some sense this is true. I believe in word because I believe abstraction is one of the unique inventions of home sapiens. In fact I would say language, abstraction, spirituality, will form a trinity of defining nature of homo sapiens. We are different from animals and other forms of being only in that we can abstract so we can create music, mathematics, language, they are all versions of abstraction. Two, we can think of a cosmic world. We can think of cosmos, which I don' think animals and birds can think of, as far as we know. And three, this notion of being interconnected, the notion of being responsible for each other, the notion that we all share, this is also very human. And these define us. This is also a spirituality in a sense. And poetry in a way serves all the three. It does serve all the three in its best moments. That is it is sensuous, affirms the world and life, two, it provokes questions and offers critique and three it always makes you feel that against all odds it is possible to be human.

12

A Time for Love, a Time for Death

RJ: Have you been influenced by the classical Sanskrit literature?

AV: I think so. I studied Sanskrit for my graduation. In fact in some ways, almost consciously perhaps or maybe not that consciously, but surely visibly I used many classical words and images which have gone out of fashion in contemporary Indian poetry, Hindi poetry particularly. And I coin words because of my knowledge of Sanskrit. Sanskrit helps a great deal there, because coinage of new words for new situation or a new feeling is possible in Sanskrit. Perhaps it is also possible in Persian, but I don't know that too much.

RJ: Some of your commentators make the analogy between classical Sanskrit drama and your poem 'Digambara'.

AV: Yes and because these images have been pushed out of our imagination. Our active contemporary imagination. So in a manner of speaking to rehabilitate them and to make them come alive again I use them, try to animate them. All poets are thieves, you know they steal from others, mostly from other poets.

RJ: But they are uncorrupted thieves.

AV: Yes they do it without a sense of performing any criminal act, without **mens rea**. They are not making anybody bereft, it is not as if you steal and the other person loses. I steal from Kalidas but it is not that Kalidas loses, anything; it is only I who gain.

RJ: When I read your poetry I feel both a sense of optimism and a sense of pessimism. There is a painful awareness of the emptiness of the world, but at the same time one can find glorious moments of optimism, about the world, about nature and about human beings.

AV: Well I don't. I would perhaps describe this as a duality in my consciousness. Between reality and possibility, the reality sometimes is very depressing. And possibility creates a realm of hope. One is a realm of hopelessness and despair, the other is a realm of hope and

Talking Poetry. Ramin Jahanbegloo, Oxford University Press. © Ramin Jahanbegloo 2022.
DOI: 10.1093/oso/9780192869180.003.0013

you cannot easily decide. You know one cannot describe a human being as an optimist or a pessimist because that kind of extremity is very rare. In Gandhi, for instance, there are moments of great hope and there are moments of great despair and both of them exist in the same person. They existed in all the great persons one knows of. So there is not necessarily a contradiction. It is not fair to see this as a contradiction. This is a double-edged reality. At one level it promotes despair and at other levels it offers possibility and hope. And both are simultaneous. Perhaps the more decisive people would choose one way or the other. I am not so decisive. Poets cannot be decisive, they have to see this as what it is, they can hardly be decisive.

RJ: Not being decisive, but having the wish of uniting the ephemeral and the eternal.

AV: That is true. I am quite obsessed with eternity but I am quite rooted in time. At least that is what I feel. But I also strongly believe that the ephemeral alone can lead you to the eternal. That you cannot access the eternal trampling on the ephemeral. Because ultimately the eternal is an ultimate version of the ephemeral.

RJ: Where do you put love in your poetry?

AV: Well I put it as a central concern.

RJ: I mean you are not a Byron.

AV: No I am not, I am not. But as I told you right in the beginning, I have sort of been disturbed or disappointed by the kind of modernity we evolved in India largely under the Victorian value sets. It made erotic sink in the background and we covered it up in a way. I thought that this was not desirable, and we must try to retrieve, the rawness, the sizzling passion. To try to do that while it is a contemporary poem, it is also a classical poem. Now can one do this? Maybe it can be done in other fields. Zbigniew Herbert in Polish had done in relation to the wider world. I try to confine it to love, because in love it is easier, it is more intense, it is more manageable in a certain sense. I would say that between hope and despair there is a running stream of love, a running stream of lure of the world. You know at one time I had described my poetry to be seen as a eulogy of the world. I want to praise the world. I want to celebrate the world. And when you say world what do you mean—then it comes to nature, love, human relationships, arts. I had written a whole book of poems on arts. Hardly any Indian poet would have a book on arts which include painters and dancers and musicians, etc. A whole book of poems. All these constitute for me the lure of the world, the celebration of the world. But also coping with death and absence. All these, and if you divide my poetic work in all these thematics, they are permeable, they are porous. It is not as if one will rule out the other. If you were to look at the whole spectrum it is born out of a deep gratitude to the world, to language to tradition, and to imagination. After all what would gratitude mean? You are grateful to whom? It is these to which I owe my existence, as it were, as a poet, apart from my personal creativity or whatever it is. But all have been honed into something meaningful hopefully, then it is by this gratitude. I want to be read as a poet of gratitude.

RJ: Is there a synthesis and a symbiosis between mystical love and erotic love?

AV: Yes I think there is and one of the things that I constantly resent that in the modern world we seem to have lost a sense of mystery. Because largely science has created a kind of an ethos where everything ultimately is knowable and it is only a matter of time, if we don't know something now. It sounds mysterious now, it is only a matter of time, we will find out through better instrumentation, better theories, better knowledge, better research and one day we will solve the mystery. As against this notion, there is, I want to posit a notion of poetry which believes that the world is and would remain an endless mystery. That mystery cannot be solved, nor it needs to be solved. There is no need to attempt that solution. This sense of wonder of the world and this sense of mystery of the world are also two central concerns running across my poetry. They are not always obvious or all that manifest but this is the running stream and I think this also means and constitute the same lure of the world. That the world is beautiful because it is mysterious, because it is wonderful because it can be loved and because it can be imagined and because it can be dreamt, etc.

RJ: Have you been influenced by the Sufi poets?

AV: To me their peculiar mixing of the mystical and the erotic, for instance, is very interesting. They all imagine themselves to be lovers. It is deeply moving for me. Even though I know that a lot of Sufis also had rather violent careers in terms of their own religious strife etc. But be that as it may, it is an enriching aspect if the erotic and the mystical get merged into each other. I think it is an enriching and up-lifting phenomenon. Because then the love of women or men gets converted into the love of cosmos, the love of everybody, the love of god, or whatever. And that attracts me. I think it is one interesting construct of human imagination and creativity. To merge with god has been possible in poetry though in many religions god is the abso-lute other, in sematic religions particularly. Very far, distant, seventh heaven, or seventh sky, or whatever. But in case of literature, poetry, and the arts, it is this merger, where human love and the so-called spiritual love are merged. Apart from Sufis, there were other Indian traditions which have this as a desirable objective. That is why Sufism took place here. One of the reasons why it took place in this part of the world. I mean even if you take the larger Persia Rumi and Hafiz and all that tradition. There is not only a geographical proximity, there is a cultural closeness which would have created this. You can trace St. Augustine or some such elements where the erotic and the cosmic merge in some sense in Christianity also. But it never became domi-nant. There was always a lurking suspicion that this was not desirable in some ways. But here, in most Bhakti poets, this is evident and many of them were not necessarily aware of the Sufis. Surdas or Tulsidas were not particularly aware, and yet they created a poetry in which the spiritual and the erotic merged, almost inevitable to each other. This became a part of the Indian tradition in a certain sense which was also rooted in reverence for all beings, a reverence also for nature, rivers, forests, etc. This sense of reverence, this sense of lure, the sense of mystery, the sense of wonder, the sense of love, they have become so rare in the human life now that perhaps one of the jobs of poetry should be to rehabilitate them in some way and bring them back to human imagination. It would be a radical act.

RJ: Yes, next to all these senses in your poetry there is a sense of lament also, you know towards the pain of the world. Poems like Auschwitz and others ... different phases of your life, express that very acutely.

AV: If I am there to sort of think in these terms and divide my poems, sometimes they are love letters to the world, as it were, sometimes they are prayers, though not to any god, sometimes they are laments and sometimes there are screams or cries. These are different ranges of emotions I am dealing with and sometimes I get very agitated. But these are all forms of poetry. What is important is what does poetry do, whether it laments or it celebrates or it prays or it screams, these are kind of different ways of expressing the same world and we are caught in this world, caught in this time, caught in the throws of eternity, battling with history.

RJ: So, you do believe that words could save us from destruction?

AV: Yes I think so. There is absolutely no intellectual basis for this, I know that, but I suspect intellect. I doubt whether intellect can explain everything, or strengthen everything. I esteem intellect but it is also nice to have occasions where you can leave the intellect behind and move to other areas. Words can take you there, they may not save but they would make you realize that it is so foolish, unnecessary to destroy the world, the earth which is beautiful, mysterious, full of eternal possibilities.

I wish to add something here. I think we have seen all too often we are so obsessed with success that we overlook the fact that many a time significance lies in failure and not in success. A poet ideally is an animal who is willing to fail! Of late, in the Indian circumstances which are politically very volatile and aggressive, social strife which is ridden by mutual hatred and divisiveness, a democratic ethos which is being usurped by majoritanism, poetry is bound to fail. My latest poetry tries to map contours of failure. There may be some nobility in failure rather than in being either silent or complicit. Poetry today must resist and risk failure.

PART III
PAINTING AND POETRY

13

Painting and the Perception of the World

RJ: Today I would like to have a conversation about painting. When we talk about painting we refer to the art of seeing. If we say that seeing comes before writing, we can say that painting comes before poetry. Would you say that painting is the first art of the human race?

AV: The historical evidence would suggest that painting was the first form of artistic articulation. The cave paintings, the primitive paintings that have been discovered, both in India and in some places in France and elsewhere, suggest that during the prehistoric period thousands of years ago, we have no remnants of any linguistic articulation, but we have painterly expression. So it seems almost certain that the first expression in terms of art was in painting and that painting preceded poetry.

RJ: But it is the perception of the world which establishes the self in the world, while poetry is more an explanation of the world because we explain the world with words. However, painting unlike poetry is not necessarily an explanation of the world. Painting is a feeling of the world.

AV: One can argue both ways. One can argue that many a time a painting is a version, a visual version of what might have disturbed or excited someone with a verbal rhythm or image or word or whatever. Sometimes the verbal gets transformed into the visual. In case of certain known cases of artists, certainly, this is true. But this does not mean the verbal is necessarily the precursor. Both ways the experience of the world, whether it is visual or verbal, is transformed into an artwork, whether it is a poem or a painting or whatever. What is important, I think, is that the world has to be there to be felt, to be sensed, to be apprehended, to be understood, to be articulated, to be commented upon. The world is important in that sense. And I have been very fond of saying that poetry and the arts are a celebration

Talking Poetry. Ramin Jahanbegloo, Oxford University Press. © Ramin Jahanbegloo 2022.
DOI: 10.1093/oso/9780192869180.003.0014

of the world, they cannot exist without the world. One can exist in some kind of a void, like the Rishis and such other spiritual kinds of persons. But that is a very rare phenomenon. I am talking of the more accessible artistic areas. The world is important just as language is important, whether it is verbal or visual or language of music or dance or gesture or whatever, language is important. Without language arts are not possible. There are two kinds of polarities that arts need to be animated into action and life: one is language and the other is the world with all its mysteries, wonders, contradictions, etc. Until they both exist art cannot take place. You can say that in the larger sense life governs both. In that case other than in life, art is not possible. There is no evidence that existence, those forms of existence which are not life, has any art.

RJ: This relation between art and life has been defined differently by different philosophers. For example a philosopher like Hegel places poetry higher than music. While Schopenhauer does exactly the opposite.

AV: That's true. But the point is, in a manner of speaking, the philosopher may choose one in comparison to the other and emphasize one element rather than the other. But a poet need not necessarily make that either/or choice. For him or her whatever or whoever, the other is equally important. It can be said in case of music the what and the how merge. So nobody really talks about what music says because maybe music does not say anything. Music can just be. Being itself is enough. Whereas perhaps the other forms of artistic expression like theatre or visual arts or poetry, they are all burdened with this notion of saying something. The usual question they face: what is it all about? A poem is about love or about nature or death, a painting is about this or that. But you don't usually ask this question about music. Music is about itself; it need not be about anything else. This idea that one can be about oneself will not usually apply to poetry or the visual arts. It has been said and argued by some philosophers or aestheticians that art must aspire to reach the condition of music because then it can supersede thin nagging question—what is it about. It can be about itself.

RJ: Would you say that the way we see things is affected by what we know or we believe?. The same phenomenon is seen differently by people because they have different beliefs.

AV: Yes I believe that there is no such thing as naked seeing, uninfluenced or pure seeing. Our belief, our notions tend to play a role, make us see what we want to see because we are used to seeing those kinds of things. But it many times prevent us from seeing what we may not have seen. One of the functions of arts in general is to bring to your attention that which in the normal course of things you may not notice or pay adequate attention to. Maybe a combination can also work. For instance, you have an apple and maybe a jar or a plate or something, these may be very work-a-day images, but you don't quite see them in that kind of a configuration, you don't see them in relation to each other and having some kind of a colour, rhythm, or lack of it or having a kind of an unspoken dialogue, being together in that sense. What art is doing, if you see a still life, is to bring to your attention a new meaning in something you might have thought to be a conventional thing, nothing to bother about or pay attention to.

RJ: But don't you think that there is a uniqueness in every work of art which is related to the uniqueness of the time and the place where it resides. For example, I would say Michelangelo's Chapel Sistine has a place and a time. I cannot imagine Chapel Sistine at the Pragati Maidan.

AV: Yes we, in the Indian tradition, had a concept of desh and kaal—desh meant space and location, and kaal meant time. So two determinants—one what is the time, is it the 10th century, it is morning or evening, is it a time when this is happening and that is not happening so this is one way—time. And the other is location/space. Where is it? Is it in a temple or a church or in an open space or a neutral space a social setting or a private place these two will determine not only the way art is created but also the way it is understood, imbibed, or reacted to by others. I remember a long time ago in a conference in Tokyo, there was a Pilipino writer who said, if to the farmers of Philippines you put up a Picasso painting, even if it is a great painting, they will fail to respond. Because it is out of context for them. They would not find any meaning in it or have any communication with it. This is because the place is different. On the other hand if they are given some orientation, some kind of an initiation into the art practice, into the modern and the moment it started, then maybe they are able to see the point. Otherwise not. So there is a deep cultural context in which art takes place. You cannot imagine in the Vatican a Khajuraho temple with sculptures of lovemaking couples. Vatican is a holy place, so is Khajuraho. But one would not imagine these kinds of lovemaking couples would be accepted at the Vatican Church. Because of the fact that the dichotomy between the spiritual and the sensuous is deeply entrenched in some of those traditions, whereas they are not so here in India, at least neither in ancient nor in medieval India. So text is critically dependent on context.

14

The Poetry of Indian Music

RJ: For example, in the Indian music, the feeling in the morning ragas is different from the feeling in the evening ragas.

AV: This is a notion prevalent in North Indian classical music. In the South there is no such thing as evening raga or morning raga. The same raag in Carnatic music is not bound by a specific time. You have this kind of a convention in the north. But again it creates a context, because people have been used to hearing Bhairavi in the early morning or late evening or Darbari in the late evening or Lalit in the morning so they tend to associate with those specifics. There has been an argument that the notes are particularly well-honed in the morning and they are rather spread out in the evening, etc. It can be argued both ways. This is a kind of convention so this convention also creates a kind of context that illuminates or informs the text. Since such a convention does not exist in the Carnatic music in the South it does not create a context.

RJ: Since we were talking about the Italian paintings of the Renaissance, I want to make a comparison with the wall paintings in India. Though there is a very strong tradition of wall painting in India. The Indian wall paintings result from a strong element of diversity in land and in faith. What has been the impact of this great heritage of India on Indian poets like yourself?

AV: India has undergone, the Indian creativity and imagination have undergone certain desirable transformations and certain undesirable interruptions and disjunctions. For instance, in both classical India and mediaeval India, literature and the arts were together, sharing the same symbology, the same repertoire of imagery, the same leitmotifs, the same narratives, etc. In poetry and visual arts, in music and in dance as well. With the intervention of the so-called modern which was largely induced by an encounter with the West, the colonizing

Talking Poetry. Ramin Jahanbegloo, Oxford University Press. © Ramin Jahanbegloo 2022.
DOI: 10.1093/oso/9780192869180.003.0015

West, some serious changes took place. Music and dance became 'classical', poetry, theatre, visual arts became 'modern'. They parted company in a certain sense. And all attempts of various kinds including my own lifetime attempts at bringing them back together, have not succeeded. Not in bridging those disruptions and distances. You may find occasional references in poetry to wall paintings, on Ajanta frescoes, Khajuraho sculptures. There are some poems about Bhimbetka, the big complex of primitive rock art. But if you were to generalize from them it would be a mistake. Unfortunately, little of Indian poetry now is responding or is in some way aware of the visual aesthetic richness of what constitutes the Indian heritage.

RJ: What about yourself?

AV: As for me, I have been considering arts (music, dance, visual arts) as a very enriching and creative neighbourhood for my poetry. Unlike almost any other Indian poet, I have a whole book of poems on arts and artists. It is entitled 'Light Creates a Temple'. Just as the modern Indian poet should not disinherit the erotics, she should not be unaware of the magnificent presence of arts in the world, in India. For me, the contemporaneous presence of the arts of my time has mattered more than the past art of heritage. In my case the resonances of heritage are more through the images that I use, through some of the words and some of the rhythms, etc.

15

Painter and Poets

A Celestial Friendship

RJ: As we saw poets are affected by painters, but how are painters influenced by poets?

AV: Well there has been a long relationship between poetry and painting, between poets and painters. In fact in the 17th, 18th, and 19th centuries a lot of miniature paintings used poetry on the canvas itself. So words constituted a form within the painting. It was a firmly entrenched convention which convention got lost or forgotten in the modern times. There are very few to recall it. Raza is one of them who tried to resurrect that in some sense by using lines of poetry on his canvas. He is the one who did the largest number of such canvases. During the struggle of the modern in Shanti Niketan, there were Rabindranath, Abaninndranath, and Nandlal Bose, all deeply immersed in literature and poetry as well. Many of the images that they had of India were basically intimations from poetic sources. They were a part of the poetic imagination from which they were inspired into visual form. Under the Marxist influence some other trends like progressive literature, a new theatre ensemble IPTA—Indian People Theatre Association was formed in Bombay in the 1940s which had musicians, theatre artists, dancers, painters, and poets come together. This was one major attempt, to bring arts together. It didn't last long. The condition is such now that might be individual friendships here and there, but you cannot say that the poets today know much about what is happening in painting or painters, for that matter, know much about what is happening in poetry. The chance encounters or personal friendships emerge but as an ethos they don't exist. They are no longer powerfully or sensuously related as they ought to be, as they had in

Talking Poetry. Ramin Jahanbegloo, Oxford University Press. © Ramin Jahanbegloo 2022.
DOI: 10.1093/oso/9780192869180.003.0016

the past both in classical and in mediaeval times. Unfortunately they have ceased to in our times.

RJ: Would you distinguish between calligraphy and the art of drawing letters. Let us not forget that calligraphy is one of the highest arts in the Islamic tradition.

AV: I would say that perhaps they both came from the same impulse. The impulse is centred around the verbal or the word. In fact several traditions including Christian. 'In the beginning was the Word': In India there has been a concept of Vak which was central. Everything emanated from Vak, from word, speech. The word, the script can itself be artistically handled which is one of the basic impulses in art creating and art practice. Script, in any case, is a visual device to record the verbal. In case of Islam, it came in handy because image-making was not permissible. So you could make the name of God in verbal signs. Because of a certain, shall we say, restriction, a religious limitation created a form of art where the two were combined. It's a beautiful magic, it has produced great art, no doubt about it. On the other hand, in the Indian situation there is a long tradition where the primacy of the word has been recognized and where there is interdependence and dialogical sort of proximities in the arts, literature, and poetry. In music a lot of poetry is used, so also in dance. Poetry does not merely exist in poetry, it is also used in paintings. So it assumes a different dimension. It is not exactly a parallel to calligraphy. There is calligraphy in China, in Japan, in Korea which again is not because of any religious requirement, but because these languages have chosen scripts which are less of script more of ideograms. More of little pictures, more of visual pictures of words. So there is the other kind of calligraphy. It does not have any particular religious meaning or any religious obligation under which they have evolved calligraphy. But in any case, either way, great art has been possible through calligraphy. But the art in India has little to do with either of these traditions. Our scripts also have a visual quality which is quite remarkable. In fact sometimes you see Hebrew or Arabic scripts, they themselves have a certain visual quality, a visual presence which is quite magical.

RJ: Many philosophers and writers have written about painting as the essence of Being. We have thinkers and writers like D.H. Lawrence and Heidegger. I was reading the other day an article by D.H. Lawrence who believes that Cezanne's painting of apples is an attempt to let the apple exist by its own separate identity. How would you say that a poet can give a separate identity to the apple?

AV: Well one of the themes my poetry has had been this relationship between the human and the non-human existence, about very ordinary things. I have a series of poems on baskets, buckets, umbrellas, shoes, etc. which are around, which we use and we see but hardly notice. One of my existential anxieties has been that while we tend to think that we are seeing these things, we never for a moment imagine that things are also seeing us, that we are also surrounded by inanimate objects which are also watching us. How to get that watchfulness of the inanimate into the animation of language has been one of the aesthetic problems I have tried to deal with. Again in the Indian tradition when it was said that the entire universe was sacred then what was sacred was not merely the living things: the animals or birds, the trees were sacred and all kinds of other objects which are otherwise inanimate are also sacred. This notion of sacredness in a manner restrained one from violating their purpose, their existence. It meant you should respect things as they are. In the current climate of instrumentalism, everything has to be seen as an instrument and you hardly respect the distinctness, the being of these objects. In fact now this insensitivity has grown about environment also. Erosion, assault, and destruction of environment on the one level and concern for effort to save environment from such assault, both these are taking place simultaneously. But what succeeds more often in terms of marketability, in terms of usage, instrumental usage, is that environment is suffering huge damage. The belief that things in the world are meant to be used by homo sapiens. This attitude itself is in some sense inhuman. In any case it does not have the sanction of Indian tradition behind it.

16

Poetry and Mediocrity

RJ: Do you see a conflict between the human reason and the human in-
tuition? It seems to me that when we are more intuitive towards the
world we are less dominating and when we are rationalizing the
world, like science and technology do, we become very dominating.

AV: The point is that knowledge can be used in many different ways. You
cannot forget the fact that knowledge is also an instrument of power,
of domination, of hegemony. That is what the Western knowledge
has done in a big way. By calling itself universal, by dominating other
forms of knowledge with this rational instrumentalism, and starting
to make knowledge itself an instrument rather than a discovery. On
such a large scale. It gives a massive illusion that home sapiens are ordained to dominate the earth.

RJ: I am interested to know if we can say that painters are more intuitive
than rational and poets are more rational than intuitive?

AV: Well I can't make that kind of a neat distinction. Because poets use,
what one may call, some kind of an emotional intelligence. But it is intelligence. It is not as if they leave their intellect aside. In good poetry
everything would be put into action. But the poetic mind is not a rational mind only. It would not be putting things in specific categories,
to view them. A poet's job is to put it all together. Not so much by
analysis but by an intuitive synthesis in which each thing finds a place.
Each poet could be different. But the so-called distinction between
the heart and the mind stands demolished. The heart is the mind and
the mind is the heart. I mean your sensitivity and your intelligence
cannot act separately or in opposition, they are not separate. That is
where good poetry would have all these elements neatly put in an integrated way. In fact mediocre poetry will not have such integration.
It is fragmented: some element will look dominant for a moment and
then subside. This does not happen in good poetry, great poetry.

Talking Poetry. Ramin Jahanbegloo, Oxford University Press. © Ramin Jahanbegloo 2022.
DOI: 10.1093/oso/9780192869180.003.0017

RJ: What is mediocre poetry?

AV: There is a lot of it, the mediocre does not discover or startle with some new discovery, either of form or of experience. But they are always in majority. The list would be very long. All you remember in romantic poetry is Wordsworth, Coleridge, Shelly, Keats, Byron, 5. But there must have been 500 poets. They were all mediocre of one kind or the other. When we talk about poetry or art, we tend to forget that we are talking about the best of them. We are not even talking about the whole of them, because we tend to segregate the best from the rest. And already the best is much smaller in numbers.

RJ: Did they decide to be the best?

AV: I don't think one can decide to be the best, although a lack of ambition is not necessarily a virtue to be hated. Poets, like any other, should better be ambitious. But poets who want to be the best may not land up being the best. They might imagine themselves to be the best, but they may not be. Lord Tennyson, if we go back to English literature, must have thought he had all the reasons to think—he was a Lord, he was a laureate, etc. And, as Auden famously said—nobody in English language knew the value of every single vowel as well as Tennyson. But after that knowledge, what he produced was not great poetry. It is at best good poetry. I'm sure Lord Tennyson wanted himself to be acknowledged as a great poet, at least as good as Coleridge and Wordsworth but surely he failed to be that. Among the moderns, Auden, Stephen Spender, Louis MacNeice, etc. One can say Auden was the best in the lot and Spender and MacNeice wrote some good poems. But they did not become masters like Yeats or Eliot. I do not know if they lacked ambition. I have no evidence to believe that. But ambition must be in keeping with one's talent, capacities, courage, and imaginative powers. Merely thinking big does not make you big.

RJ: Gertrude Stein believed that a painter can never write and a writer can never paint. Did you ever try to paint?

AV: No I didn't. I would say that each has a separate valuable domain. Some people can paint and they would be good at it; there are people who can write and they would be good at it. Once in a while, here and there, one of them tries the other thing. So Picasso has written poems. Several of these painters, especially during the surrealistic phase, did write poetry but they did not aspire to become poets. Similarly, some poets may have tried their hand at painting but I don't think anyone of them became a painter of consequence. I think the coming together may sometimes be interesting. It may bring out some temporary nice feeling and result, but in the end what one is what one should be, rather than trying to be both.

17

The Magical World of Raza

RJ: But what brought you so close to a painter like Raza?

AV: I was a young man and a student at St. Stephens College Delhi from a small town. I used to feel I have not attained sufficient cultural literacy. I used to visit every concert, play, exhibition, poetry reading, literary seminar, just to educate myself. It was a deep feeling of trying to know. And as I went along I started feeling there is something different here, something that is we who practice words cannot do. What the colours can do, visual shapes can do, words cannot do. But by the same token, what words can do, the colours and other shapes cannot. So after having felt and experienced all this, as a civil servant when I went back to Madhya Pradesh, my home state I started looking for culture in a more integrated manner. I was posted in tribal districts with large number of tribals who had their own art, whereas I had never imagined that they had anything by way of art. In their case the same person who dances, sings, makes the instrument, plays on the instrument, perhaps composes the verses. There was no individual assertion, no stress on individual identity: everything was community and group-based. This was a very different approach from what we were used to and what we were trained in. When I came to Bhopal and in addition to my other duties I was put in charge of the State Academy of Visual and Performing Arts I started seeing a little more carefully, a little more intently, and a little more professionally. And in that context I started inviting important painters to come and do one-man shows. So M F Husain, Ram Kumar, Akbar Padamsee, J Swaminathan, Vivan Sundaram, Sudhir Patvardhan, Nalini Malani, etc. showed. And in the same series Raza from Paris came. Raza belonged to Madhya Pradesh. He was in France for many decades. Seeing all of them, their works, so different from each other, their view points, their aesthetics, their political standpoints, etc., I realized

Talking Poetry. Ramin Jahanbegloo, Oxford University Press. © Ramin Jahanbegloo 2022.
DOI: 10.1093/oso/9780192869180.003.0018

there was quite an intense, passionate irrepressible, and creative plurality. That became my obsession, in a manner of speaking. Plurality is the essence of existence and creativity. It turned out that Raza seemed to be very deeply interested in poetry which I had never anticipated or imagined. He attended a poetry reading session and took copious notes. I gave him in 1979 the only book of poems that I had published so far. He took it and a little later in Paris he did a painting inscribing a line of one of my poems. The line he used is 'Mother when I return, what shall I bring? Originally this was more of a lament for failure, that I was sent here to do something and I was not able to do it, now if I came back, what was going to happen? What could I bring? Raza, on the other hand, used this as a letter to his country, homeland. So he extended the meaning to mean the mother country. I was writing to my mother, my physical mother but then the meaning got changed. I started realizing that a painter, who is sensitive to poetry, may use poetic words in a different way. Raza was deeply interested. In fact it was around 1980, before that, all his titles were English or more importantly, French. But henceforward he started giving titles mostly in Hindi and they were very poetic. Sometimes he would ring me up from Paris and say, I am doing this kind of a painting and I want to call it this, is this the right word or can you suggest some other word, etc. Those were the times when a long friendship between us, a poet and a painter started. Later some official work or the other would take me to Europe attending conferences, etc. and I would make it a point to go to Paris and meet him. So it got closer and whenever he would come to India, I would invite him to Bhopal. When I moved to Delhi, during all his visits to Delhi we would unfailingly meet. I retired from Civil Service in 2001 and he started insisting that I should spend more time in Paris with him. For many years I used to stay with him for several weeks in winter and in summer, to be with him, chat, see him work, do my work. It became a very close friendship. He was interested in Gandhi, he was interested in many different things like poetry, music, spirituality, etc., and, he always wanted to know what was happening in India, what people were thinking in the world of arts, poetry, culture, etc.

RJ: Why did Raza decide to live and work in Paris?

AV: As a young painter, he was showing in Srinagar, Kashmir. And it so
   happened that in 1948 I think, Henri Cartier Bresson, the great French
   photographer, was visiting Srinagar and happened to see Raza's show.
   He told him, 'Young man you have talent but your painting lacks construction. You should study Cezanne.' That was his advice. Raza then
   argued with him—What do you mean by construction; What do you
   mean by saying that a painting is constructed? Cartier Bresson explained that a painting was like a building, it had to be built—foundation, basement, etc. Raza came back to Bombay and he started
   wondering, how could he see Cezanne? Some of Cezanne's works
   were reproduced in some books. But that was not enough he said
   to himself: Why don't I try to go to France on a Scholarship, see and
   study Cezanne? He learnt French (Alliance Française) and appeared
   for an interview. He had started speaking French well by that time and
   he got the scholarship for two years. He landed up in Paris. He entered
   a conventional school of art there. There he met his would-be wife.
   His entire family had left including his first wife, for Pakistan, after
   partition. He had been alone for many years. They decided to marry.
   Raza won in 1956 a prestigious prize chosen by art critics of 17 French
   newspapers. He was the first non-European to be given that award.
   That established him and he could get a reasonable income from his
   art. Since his wife was the only child of her parents naturally, Raza
   did not want that they should come away to India leaving her parents
   behind in France. Another consideration was that they both being
   professional painters, they decided that they would not have a child.
   They lived together from 1959 to 2004. She was a substantial painter
   herself. When she died in 2004 he was all by himself and I started per-
   suading him to come back. He wanted to, he would visit India, he was
   very attached to India, he never changed his passport, did not take
   French nationality though he lived in France for nearly 60 years.
RJ: Yes, he is very French, but at the same time he has an Indian sensibility.
AV: He used to say that how to paint I learnt from France, but what to
   paint I learnt from India. He had a tremendous sense of colour, ex-
   uberance, rhythm, orchestration, richness, nuances, possibilities
   of colour. He was acknowledged as a master colourist. Then, in the
   1970s, he started questioning himself: I have become a painter of

Parisian school, where is India in this? Where is Raza in this? Then he started evolving his own style. For him the world was a mystery and the job of the artist was to keep on addressing this beautiful, complex mystery that the world is. I used to tell him. You are a painter of origins, you are not looking at history, you are looking at eternity. What is eternal, what is essential, what is original, rather than what is soiled and damaged and transformed by history. For him, time did not matter in that sense. In the sense that you are reacting to your time, that did not matter.

18

Being and Nothingness

RJ: I read an interview with Raza where he describes his painting as a process of becoming. Becoming is a concept that you find among many philosophers. However, I believe that Raza's painting is somewhere between nothingness and being.

AV: For him objects did not matter. Some figurative work he did in the beginning, like everybody else, but then he gave up that. He hardly painted figurative work. I think in his case colours were primary. I used to watch him in his studio sometimes and the way he sometimes suddenly created by mixing a new hue, a new colour kind of a colour you did not expect. His eyesight was, towards the end, quite weak. But he would create a colour which was amazing. I have sometimes said that his paintings were like prayers which were offered in a manner of asking for grace. On the other hand, they were addressed to himself, he was not talking to anybody: he was talking to himself, but not in a sense of self-indulgence, nor in a sense of self-escape. Self should wither away. What should remain is the art-object itself. So in a manner of speaking you can come back to what we talked earlier—the object itself. Here was not an object which existed outside the work, not in the objective world, it exists within the aesthetic world. It has been created by it and that's it. It is not describing or reproducing anything that exists somewhere, he is creating it. In that process the object, the artwork comes into existence.

RJ: Was he satisfied with his painting?

AV: Well he had both satisfaction and dissatisfaction, like a true honest, self-critical artist. He would once in a while say you know it did not seem to be all that bad. Sometimes he would say he made a big mistake: 'I don't know what I am doing?' The canvas would be lying there. It was not as if he would have not thought about it. He would start and then everything would start falling in place not necessarily as

Talking Poetry. Ramin Jahanbegloo, Oxford University Press. © Ramin Jahanbegloo 2022.
DOI: 10.1093/oso/9780192869180.003.0019

thought. It happens with writing also, sometimes you feel there is a block and then it evaporates once you take to pen. He had a certain playfulness the element of Leela; the element of thinking through Leela. You are playing and through that play you are reflecting. There is a deep reflective element which is not very conscious but which is not fully unconscious either. It is not happening all by itself but there is spontaneity, which I think the medium brings, which is the medium of colour. The colour then supersedes ideas and other things and takes over and the colour creates being that is like becoming. It's a becoming of colours from whatever has provoked its being.

RJ: Do you believe that India can produce another Raza?

AV: I do not see the possibility. For many reasons—One of them happens to be that the climate has changed and circumstances have changed. I think there is such overriding cultural amnesia now that it will be very difficult for someone to cut the crap and reach to the essence. Also, many new styles and other forms of expression have come in. Many new ways of looking at and celebrating the world have come in. Raza was a very skilled aesthete. He thought that the world was beautiful and he can add a bit to that enormous beauty. Many of our later day artist friends do not think they are creating beauty; beauty is not their concern and they don't think the world is beautiful. Not anymore.

PART IV

THE PASSION FOR MUSIC

19

The Art of Being an Indian Musician

RJ: Let us talk about Indian music, which has played an important role in your life. How did you get interested in music in general? Was it just as an amateur listener?

AV: As a young boy and a school student I was interested in popular and film music and at that time we had two great popular singers, K.L. Sehgal and Lata Mangeshkar universally admired. I also used to follow and imitate them. One day, by accident, I happened to attend my first Indian classical music concert, being held in my small central Indian town Sagar. I had no background, in fact, I had no interest in staying on. I went out of a young man's curiosity to know what this classical music was all about? I had decided with a friend of mine, we both were poets, that we would stay there for 15 minutes and move on. A tall handsome looking man with a very strong powerful voice was singing. And I got stuck, and ended up listening to him for the next two hours! It occurred to me, this was music. What were three and a half minute songs which films used to have? And that evening I turned to this music for my life as a listener. There were very few occasions for such music in Sagar. Luckily all India Radio at that time used to organize classical music concerts in different cities. One such concert was organized in Sagar when I was a student at the University and I attended it. Then I started listening to classical music concerts on the radio which by then had already emerged as a major forum for disseminating classical music and also a major patron of many of the classical musicians who had been rendered jobless after the princely states merging in India. Then I moved to Delhi to study in St. Stephen's and was in Delhi for 5 years, 1960–65. During that period there wasn't a classical music concert in this city, whether Hindustani music or Carnatic music or Western music which I did not attend. It became almost a habit. Even in Sagar once I was hearing a recital by Ustad Ali

Talking Poetry. Ramin Jahanbegloo, Oxford University Press. © Ramin Jahanbegloo 2022.
DOI: 10.1093/oso/9780192869180.003.0020

Akbar Khan on Sarod. Suddenly because of the time slot available on the radio was of half an hour, the music stopped. My youngest sister was trying to climb the stairs to the room where I was sitting and listening to this music. The moment the music stopped I looked and found that she was struggling to keep her hand clutch the banister. The two got connected in my mind. I wrote a poem in two parts on Ali Akbar Khan's Sarod playing and I used the image of Orpheus. The stopping of the music was as if Orpheus had looked back at Eurydice whom he had brought from the land of death. He had committed himself that he would not look at her until they reached the Earth. But just as they were reaching the Earth, he could not resist the temptation to look back at his beautiful wife and she disappeared as ordained by the death god. I used all these images for that sudden stopping. So music became in fact in a certain manner a creative theme. It has been like that for a long time. I have written poems on many musicians. I came in close contact with some great vocalists of our time. More importantly, Kumar Gandharv and Mallikarjun Mansur. In fact, I wrote my longest poem consisting of a group of 21 independent poems on the death of Kumar Gandharva, a kind of requiem. Music became both a source of pleasure and reflection when I joined civil service in Madhya Pradesh, I became a major organizer of classical music concerts, seminars, festivals, etc.

RJ: So, like many Indians you feel closer to Indian music than Western music?

AV: There are few Indians who are closer to Western than Indian music. There are many Indians who like Western classical music including some musicians as well. Yes, there are some Indians, two of my nephews, who know as much about Western music. They are twins—Asteek and Hutashan and they both know a lot about Western classical music. In fact, there was a time when I used to bring on their demand, from London or Paris, cassettes and CDs of major conductors like Karajan.

There is a major difference between the two musics; if I may say. I think the Western classical music has a linear path. You leave point A, go over to point B, move on to point C to D, never return to these points covered. In the Indian classical music it is cyclical. You leave A go to B, come back to A go to C come back to B. And you keep on

... so it's cyclical and the other thing is that primarily the Hindustani classical music and also the Carnatic are vocal. The instruments aspire to a condition of the vocal. So the highest compliment you would pay to a Sitar player or an instrument player is that in her hands an instrument almost sings. My understanding is that the Western classical music is basically instrumental. Not that there is no vocal just as not that there is no instrumental here in Indian classical music. The notion of the orchestra which is so dominant in the Western came to India but did not succeed here, in spite of some interesting experimentation in that direction. We didn't have the concept of orchestral music. Our music is very much individual-centred music. A musician has accompaniment, he may even have a co-singer, or a co-instrumentalist, but basically it is the music of an individual. Perhaps Western music, more often, is group music; not that it doesn't have a place for individuality. It certainly has. There are certain similarities also, for instance; the Western conductor will perform a particular symphony, conduct it in a particular way and create a new version from others who might have also performed it. Similarly ragas can be performed differently, the same raga, the same musician can perform differently, as many times as he feels. This is one similarity. But, on the other hand, Western music is written music, you have notations. Here it is oral, notation has come but it never took root. It was adopted from the West and some of our Pandits created notation systems. It is customary in the Western concerts to have the music sheets and they can be turned around. Here some of our outstanding singers or performers including the younger ones would never use any music sheets. The entire thing is done out of memory. So there are these differences.

20

Poetizing Ragas

RJ: There are many similarities between Persian music and Indian music. But as you said there is a huge difference between Western music and Indian music even in the manner of listening of the audience.

AV: Two points. One, as the Indian classical music exists now is quite indebted to Iranian or Persian music and also to Arabic music because these are two music streams which came to India when Arabs and Persians came to India. They brought this music. Also, the miniature painting came to India from Persians through the Mughals. The Indians in a very big way adopted that. Similarly in the miniature paintings there are all kinds of little details here and there, very meticulously done. Similarly in music the same kind of miniature locations within the overall structure of the raga are touched or traversed. Many of the musical terms, in fact, like Khayal, Behlawa, Mukaam, are Persian words; some of the terminologies which is used in Hindustani classical music is originally Persian. Of course, it could be different from what the Persian music may use them for. It has adopted elements but has Indianized them in a way. You cannot imagine, Indian classical music, without the fully domesticated, absorbed Persian elements. I've heard on authority of a musician that even Carnatic music has influence of Persia. So it's quite old. Everything in India is, in a way, quite old and the old is also very contemporary in some surprising ways. But the fact remains that it is not the old which is completely reproduced. It has undergone through historical processes and transformations. All the imprints of history are there on its body. It is said that it is Amir Khusro who first gave some shape to this kind of music, and that is already 13h century. So, it's through Amir, that several things seemed to have come. He wrote poetry with a line in Persian and the other in Hindi or Sanskrit. It's something which sometimes we forget, particularly in the current climate of cultural

Talking Poetry. Ramin Jahanbegloo, Oxford University Press. © Ramin Jahanbegloo 2022.
DOI: 10.1093/oso/9780192869180.003.0021

amnesia, that it is these others who brought many things to us, and we should be grateful for that, because that has enriched the native musical traditions in very strong, deep, imaginative ways.

RJ: Would you say that there is a very strong poetic element in Indian music?

AV: There is a theory, of course, that says that certain Ragas using certain combinations of notes at a particular hour of the day are more suitable for that hour than others. This operates more strictly in the Hindustani classical music. There is no such observance of timeliness in the Carnatic music. It does not follow this prescription. A Raga has a creative combination of some notes and it has been the same for centuries. Yet the rendition brings in some new elements, some new hue, some new colours. In fact the word Raga also indicates a certain, at one level—passion, but also colour. So the personality, the mood, the timing, the ambience, they all contribute to making the Raga what at that particular moment it would communicate that particular rendition is going to denote or evoke in some sense, or embody. Unlike in the Western classical music concerts when there is light only on the stage, and the hall is dark it is quite different here. Here, the audience must be seen by the performer, and the performer must have an eye-to-eye contact. The response of the audience contributes to the elaboration or the innovation or the movement of the Raga. This is unlike the Western music, where the audience plays no direct or sensuous role in the performance, except that at the end you clap. In India, it is a dialogue between the audience and the performer. And the dialogue is usually quiet, although it sometimes also assumes a certain level of sound. Otherwise, a quiet dialogue that takes place between the audience and the performer is distinct from what happens in the Western concert. The other thing which I must mention is that, perhaps, we are the only classical music which has survived the Western classical music. All other musics, Chinese and Japanese and several others have been devoured by the Western classical music. I don't know much about the middle eastern part, maybe even they have survived in spite of the impact. But the Indian classical music has survived in all its richness and complexities. In fact, one of the arguments that I had once given was, music in India resisted colonization. There are many compositions in the praise of minor kings and minor gods, and whoever. But in the Hindustani classical music there is not a single bandish or composition in the praise of the British. Not one. I am told that there are some in Carnatic music, which are not in keeping with my theory. But by and large, and I try to argue that the fact is that the Indian classical music almost did not recognize colonization, it bypassed it. Similarly, the Indian classical dance bypassed the colonization. Colonization has deep impact on literature, theatre, on visual arts. It transformed them in some ways, caused disruptions and dislocations in many ways. They were under the impact of the colonial aesthetics. But music and dance bypassed colonization. They almost ignored it!

21

Indian National Music

RJ: Are you saying that Indian classical music played a very important role in the rise of Indian nationalism?

AV: Well, at one time it did because, you know the Congress Party was the biggest forum of protest, resistance, and struggle. In the Amritsar session of the Congress top three classical vocalists were invited to perform in the presence of Mahatma Gandhi. So there must have been some acknowledgement at some level that this classical music was truly Indian and free from colonial impact. The idea of national music had not come up at the time. But classical music was playing an integrating role. Many musicians like the Carnatic vocalist MS Subbalakshmi became a national and perhaps nationalist icon. Since nothing in India is singular, and the idea of a national music, or a national dance or a national theatre based on singularity, is really not valid. There are and have been two types of Indian classical music, at least eight kinds of classical dance. Plurality is dominant in the classical realm as well. But there was definitely an attempt to assert that we exist as a people and this is our creative wealth. And this was more evident perhaps in music and dance.

RJ: Who listens today to Indian classical music: masses or elites?

AV: What has happened is very interesting. Before independence, the Hindustani classical music and Carnatic music had two kinds of patronage. One was the royal courts whether it was a Muslim nawab or a Hindu prince or rich elite they all loved to have court musicians invariably classic musicians. This is true here and this is perhaps true in Carnatic musical geography also. The other was the temples which were more active in that field and remain active even till today in the south. In the north the relationship between temples and music was disrupted and there are very few temples which would have musicians now. In the south they remain. So this was the kind of client age. In

Talking Poetry. Ramin Jahanbegloo, Oxford University Press. © Ramin Jahanbegloo 2022.
DOI: 10.1093/oso/9780192869180.003.0022

the temple it was devotees and ordinary people and in the royal court it was the elite. When freedom came and the princely states merged in the union the age-old royal patronage disappeared. There was a deep crisis of patronage. Indian classical music, then, started democratizing itself and today, it is more democratic in terms of access. It is largely free of state patronage, although part of it remains craving for and getting that patronage. At that crucial point the All India Radio which was a government institution provided the necessary refuge to these musicians who were rendered jobless, in a manner of speaking, with the abolition of the princely states. Then gradually and till today, while the bourgeoisie is one part of the clientele, younger people have been moving, towards classical music in a big way. The difference is that the times when this music developed and originated were the times when the other kinds of music were not so widespread. Today the music scene is much more complex, varied, and crowded. It has all kinds and brands of popular music, film music is a very major element and other kinds of pop music. Understandably the clientele of classical music is small compared to other popular forms of music. But in significance and in richness there is no comparison between the two. The classical is deeper, culturally more rooted, it's more civilizing in its influence on those who are vulnerable than other brands of popular music. But this music has to struggle for its place viz a viz these other kinds of music, the Western music, the Western pop music, etc. The Western music audience in this country are rather limited. It has never grown to be so big as to be either a threat or a rival to Indian classical music.

22

Tradition and Innovation

RJ: But there has been a huge influence of Western music on film music in India.

AV: Oh yes, and many millions of Indians listen to film music. Of course. For a long time film music was not taken seriously in academic and intellectual circles. Now it is being studied because it's a form which is very widespread and popular. It's important that it is studied. In literature or visual arts, classical music or classical dance the number of people who are interested in these things is limited. Democracy, unfortunately, levels everything. The claims of popularity are forever pitched against the claims of significance. Importance of complexity in a certain sense is marginalized. The popular becomes accessible. Even the classical music is also sometimes tempted to do that.

RJ: How do you see the relationship between the Indian classical music and the Indian film music? Are these two worlds deeply intertwined or ideologically opposed to each other?

AV: No, there has been a give and take. I mean film music has very little to give to the classical music but classical music has had a lot to give. In the earlier period (now it does not seem to be happening as much) in the 30s, 40s, 50s, film music was heavily borrowing from the classical music, from the Raagas, from the Bandishs, etc. Now that seems to have receded. The impact of the film music on classical music has been very thin. Sometimes some musicians think they should also do popular things. But the mainstream classicists remain uninfluenced. So the relationship is not quite symbiotic in that sense. Ideologically they are opposed to each other but both attempt to make people enjoy sound in a meaningful way. After all the classical is music through sound and film and other forms of music are also music through sound. And both are enjoyable. So there are similarities, music is music. But in terms of significance, in terms of depth, in terms of

Talking Poetry. Ramin Jahanbegloo, Oxford University Press. © Ramin Jahanbegloo 2022.
DOI: 10.1093/oso/9780192869180.003.0023

imagination, in terms of resonance of the past, the classical is far more vital. Film music is nostalgic sometimes. But it seldom has resonance of the past. The past comes alive more powerfully in the classical than in other forms of popular music.

RJ: It seems to me that the Indian traditional music resists to all forms of innovation.

AV: This is again a notion which is debatable for the following reasons: One, in India tradition and change have never been seen as a binary. In India change is located within tradition rather than outside tradition, seldom separately. I have been listening to this music for nearly 50 years, the same music, the same ragas, more or less, the same people performing. But I can feel that the music has changed. So the music can be perceived or received by those who have followed the tradition, but also by those who do not belong to that tradition. There is something new happening, something innovative. There are musicians who have innovated without ever claiming or being recognized as doing innovation. Kumar Gandharva, Malikarjun Mansoor, Ravi Shanker, Kishori Amonker, are not musicians who are mere traditionalists; they have also been innovative. Some of them openly, others quietly. It does appear that tradition admits to change. It admits innovation with difficulty, with some degree of reticence with some element which is deeply conservative. And yet tradition itself keeps on changing. In this music there is no such thing as pure tradition because several Gharanas, several schools of music, are treating the same Raag but they are doing it differently. This itself is innovation. It is the same repertoire being rendered one way by one, another way by another in different ways and so on. These different ways are clearly innovative yet remaining in the same tradition.

23

Qawwali and the Art
of Devotional Singing

RJ: If I understand you well, what you are saying is that individual compositions rely on the individual motivations.

AV: I once tried to distinguish about a great musician from a good musician, at least in the Indian context. A good musician is one who sings or performs as per the prescribed norms within the limits of the Raaga, he performs the Raaga authentically perhaps perfectly, grammatically correct. He is a good singer or a good performer. A great musician will be one who sings himself, making the Raag as a pretext. The text is himself or herself and the Raag is the pretext. So a Mallikarjun Mansur or a Kumar Gandharva does not sing a Raag; each one of them sings himself through a Raag. A great musician is a very powerful individual himself, but his own power through the Raag. You also get a new version of the Raag, and strong sense of individuality. The individual vision overwhelming the innate raag vision and coming out with a version that is unique.

RJ: Let us take the example of Qawwali. In Qawwali, you should know the tradition and follow your master, but you can also create your own unique style.

AV: In Qawwali there is the given structure and there is this freedom or licence you can grab to add to the given composition. They call it 'girah lagaana', you are using the same structure and yet in between you can deviate, bring something from elsewhere and go on. This is freedom and this is an instance of individual freedom that you can choose from elsewhere. The verse is given but within the given verse you can interpolate other verses of your choice, and you are free to do that. This is acceptable. This is very much a tradition in Qawwali.

Talking Poetry. Ramin Jahanbegloo, Oxford University Press. © Ramin Jahanbegloo 2022.
DOI: 10.1093/oso/9780192869180.003.0024

RJ: How can we explain the fact that in the past 20 years, there has been a new interest, especially in North India, in the Sufi music but not in the Sufi poetry?

AV: In modern world, for whatever reason, we all are bereft of a sense of the mystery of the universe, as it were, because a kind of a pseudo-scientific ambience has been created which makes you feel that everything can be knowable. If you don't know it, over a period of time you will come to know it. And unlike the Sufi or the other kinds of traditions which believe that there are mysteries which are unresolvable and they are so beautiful and wonderful. There is this yearning somewhere and Sufi music came to fill the gap. But poetry is a different matter. Sufi music and Sufi poetry are not coterminous. Most Sufi singers do not necessarily resort to or pick up the best Sufi poetry. What they pick up is the more fashionable, the more popular, the more accessible Sufi poetry. The more difficult and the more complex Sufi poetry is not easily accessible either to music or to understanding. You have to have certain parameters of understanding, of comprehension, then alone you can access that. So there is this difference, understandably so. What they are listening gives them a sense of the mystery. But it is at a rather superficial level. It succeeds in creating a communion of a certain kind which is not spiritually very enriching I suspect.

RJ: Maybe there is less devotion in music.

AV: In the sense that you are imbibing all this from a very secular position. So there is a block. You are not accepting it as it is, you are doing a willing suspension of disbelief for the time being. You are not really being initiated. It becomes more ritualistic or merely formal in that sense.

24

The Colours of Hindustani Classical Music

RJ: Does this have to do with the English-speaking urban audience? Maybe because they listen to music, but perhaps they don't have a deep approach to music?

AV: These are very much the shallow secular urban middle classes. In fact in the folk traditions already and even now, a lot of poetry and a lot of music exist which are deeper, which more existentially inspire and which are listened to by people in large numbers. So there is a parallel world in folk music and a large world which is unmapped and many a time unknown to us, the urban animals. And there all these elements which have gone into the fabric of the kind of music they create, where Kabir exists and folk music exists and erotic impulses exist, celebration of nature exists, questioning yourself and your mortal existence exists where God and its various forms exist, deep questioning also exists and in different ways and different forms in different manners and different regions.

RJ: I want to come back to your own relationship, as a poet, to music. I was reading an article by Ananda Coomaraswamy on Indian music. There is a passage where he mentions that an Indian singer is a poet and a poet is a singer. Very beautifully said. I just like to know if you consider yourself as a singer?

AV: I would, because a lot of the poetic structure that I have evolved over time in my poetry has something to do with musical structure. It is not written to be sung, neither I can sing it nor anybody else would. It's not set to music in that sense. But its inner music is very much

Talking Poetry. Ramin Jahanbegloo, Oxford University Press. © Ramin Jahanbegloo 2022.
DOI: 10.1093/oso/9780192869180.003.0025

the classical where the images are repeated, where there is detailing, there is this miniature kind of filling the canvas, where different kinds of colours are brought in. All these things which seem to be in my mind, I would consider to be essentially coming from my experience in music. My poetry owes a lot to Hindustani classical music.

PART V
A PLURAL INDIANNESS

25

Poet as a Dissenter

RJ: Let us talk about your Indianness. How do you situate yourself in today's world as an Indian poet? You travel a lot and you have been recently in Europe. But you always present yourself as an Indian poet. But where do poetry and Indianness meet in your life?

AV: In times like ours where, unfortunately, in India, Indianness is defined in a very parochial, narrow, hard, exclusive way, I would like to think that my Indianness is very different wide, open, plural, and inclusive. And I don't want to wear it on my sleeve. After all there is a world scenario of poetry and I locate myself humbly in that as a poet. That I am from India, of course, matters to me; it matters to me, it matters to my poetry, it even matters to those who receive me in some sense. But it is not necessarily an Indianness which can be easily discerned. But I'll give you a couple of examples. A lot of modern writing in India has been influenced by the West, whether it is colonial period or post-colonial period. We are not exactly free from that influence. And I think that influence has been in some measure creatively and intellectually enriching. So we have started looking at the world in way which was traditionally not ordained, or traditionally not available. But I have always wondered as to how is that in the Indian modern literature, the one element of Indian tradition, its celebrativeness has survived. Now a celebrative modernism will be totally unacceptable in the Western tradition where celebrative nature of poetry or literature has all been discarded, side-lined, suppressed. But in case of India it remains according to me and, in any, case I have a very strong streak in my poetry of that celebrativeness. I have been saying that after all poetry is born out of your love and lure of the world and, therefore, it is almost morally compulsive for an Indian poet to celebrate the world, to celebrate life and existence, the plurality of everything. I would say that I have read and have been influenced by some of the great modern poets like

Talking Poetry. Ramin Jahanbegloo, Oxford University Press. © Ramin Jahanbegloo 2022.
DOI: 10.1093/oso/9780192869180.003.0026

Rilke, Yeats, Eliot, Zbniew Herbert, Octovio Paz, Pablo Neruda, etc. In Latin America a bit of celebrativeness survived because their own local traditions could not be completely wiped out or demolished by the colonial experience, like in India. I could say that I locate myself where these two civilizations broadly speaking—Western Civilization and Indian Civilization come together in creative dialogue. Not necessarily in contestation or being unconcerned with each other. I locate myself in that domain. And if you remember that Polish scholar-critic Renata Czekalska, who wrote a whole book on my poetry, puts me there. It is she who for the first time acknowledged or discerned this element that I am not an Indian poet ensconced completely and comfortably in some Indian tradition or modernism. I am a poet who has also in a manner of speaking participated in the other largely Western tradition. And I am not uncomfortable with either and their meeting point.

RJ: But you also consider yourself as a dissenter. Where does dissent start and end for you as an Indian poet?

AV: Indianness itself is such a pluralistic phenomenon as I have tried to argue in my Introduction to 'Indian Dissents' that dissent is almost inevitably woven into the Indian fabric, whether it is dissent from the state or dissent from tradition, from faith or belief or values. So dissent is nothing new. Except in our understanding of it and our initiation into some aspects of Indian tradition we seem to have ignored this plurality, the plurality of dissent itself. And of existence. For instance, in the normal Indian tradition, a person who is concerned with spiritual issues will inevitably be involved with religion. In the Indian tradition it has not been possible to look at spirituality without religion. But some of us, poets like me, I would like to think, have tried to evolve a kind of spirituality which responds to the large reality, which responds to the fact that we are part of a much larger reality, a cosmic reality than the human reality alone or the social, political, or the economic reality. That there is a larger universe to which we belong and each thing in this universe is responsible for the other. Now this is basically a spiritual dimension. It is also a kind of dissent from the tradition which had kept spirituality somewhat encased in religion. Some of us writers, however, have moved away from that encasement within religion to a more open space where spirituality can exist without religion. Somebody could even make a claim that we have liberated spirituality from the clutches of religion. I don't know if this is too tall a claim to be made, but such claim may have some validity.

26

Walking in the Steps of the Mystics

RJ: You have been walking in the steps of the mystics.

AV: Since I said there has been a space for dissent within Indian traditions, the connection with mystics and the connection with other dissenters are inevitable.

RJ: Would you say that Indians talk about their traditions in relation to their present needs of the present or as legitimate institutions of the past?

AV: I would say while the presence and relevance of Indian tradition to India cannot be denied, nor possibly be objected to, no tradition, whether Indian or any other, could be, in such a complex evolving world, be completely a matter of the past. Past is important, the presence of past in our present is also relevant and can be felt, but past cannot claim to have found all the answers for everything, for us already. There are huge number of problems, issues, and concerns which would have never arisen before. Look at this issue of right to privacy, there is no evidence in our traditions, whether a person has this inalienable right. Because according to the Dharmic traditions and others, your rights are subject to divine commitment and divine intervention. Therefore while it is possible to find some echo in the past of many of the issues, problems, and complexities that arise in the modern times in India, they cannot be adequately addressed nor explained in terms of something in the past. In any case, traditions in India have to be renewed, rejuvenated through expansion and change.

RJ: But when we are talking about the past, we are talking about historical memory. How much of this historical memory is present in your work as a poet?

AV: For me memory is very important. For me even racial memory is important. I think we the homo sapiens are uniquely blessed with both memory and language and these are the two critical factors for

Talking Poetry. Ramin Jahanbegloo, Oxford University Press. © Ramin Jahanbegloo 2022.
DOI: 10.1093/oso/9780192869180.003.0027

literature or the arts, poetry, etc. Memory would also mean a kind of inheritance. It is not something you have earned yourself, at one level. At another level these memories have also been formalized in certain ritualistic structures and these structures are not necessarily reviving or revitalizing memory. Many a time these ritualistic structures actually impede memory in its genuineness, in its spontaneity. In other words, there is both a history of memory and a politics of memory. Thus one has to be very careful. For me, for instance, memory would not only consist of what happened in history, the so-called socio-political history, it is also what happens in literature, in ideas, in thought, what happened to the earlier writers and what happened to our creative imaginative ancestors and what is happening to us. If we are able to correlate it sometimes, through a metaphor, through an image, whatever—it illuminates both. It illuminates the contemporary and also the past. Both are illuminating each other at the best moment, which may or may not happen all that often.

RJ: Are we talking about a plural memory which produces plural poetry? In India, we have different forms of poetry: we have spiritual poems, secular nationalistic poems, Sufi poems, etc.

AV: Indian memory can't but be plural. We have talked about this before, India by definition is plural. In memory, just as in imagination, in ideas, in articulation, in expression. So it is a plurality cutting across. Memory is even a matter of choice, what you chose. You can choose in fact something from the past plurality and the choice would be determined by what you are trying to look at. There is in that sense a politics of choice. I don't know what other words to use. The issue is why are you choosing this and not that? In a civilization that is so many thousand years old, your choice of plurality itself is so big and rich that what you chose out will also determine what you are looking at. From a great epic like Mahabharatha, you can choose what is happening on the battlefield when Krishna is trying to persuade Arjun and trying to explain what Dharma is. On the other hand, you can look at Mahabharatha as a counterpoint to Ramayana. In Ramayana, the 'dharmayudha', the righteous war triumphs and finally a very humane regime is established. In Mahabharatha on the other hand, a similar dharmayudha is fought but there is no victor and it seems all wars are fought in vain and they never achieve anything except violence. If you are looking at it this way you are reaching a different point. All this is legitimate memory. It is possible in our times particularly, what we are suffering in India today, what we are going through in India today, it is very important what we choose. Because memories are being chosen in a manner where they tend to cloud out many other memories. If you look at the historical narration, as it goes these days, you can look at Muslims as aggressors and nurture a sense of retrospective outrage. This is one way of looking at history. Another way of looking at history is that although their early ancestors came as aggressors, they adopted this land. After all, Mughals did not go anywhere, they settled here and most of the Mughal kings were born here, barring the first one. Mughals became Indians. That is another way of looking at it. It is the same history, the same memory. It makes all the difference as to what are you trying to look at, what is your concern in invoking memory. Memory in poetry can work in many different ways. It can illuminate a certain contemporary reality by connecting it to something that might have happened earlier of akin nature, it can create a counterpoint to a contemporary experience, it can create an interrogative space where both memory and reality are questioned within the space of the poem. And it can, of course, create mass hysteria, which will not be in keeping with the moral nature of the job of poetry. Memory cannot ignore the complex plurality of history for it to be authentic, human, and enriching.

27

A Son of Ghalib and Kabir

RJ: Considering this plural memory, do you see yourself as a son of Ghalib, Kabir, or Amir Khusro?

AV: I would say that could be the lineage. But this would be kind of a self-validating action, I claim as my inheritance, the Vedic, the Upanishadic, the great Sanskrit literature, the Buddhist wisdom, and the Samyak, you know the middle path. But I also claim the dissidence of a Kabir or the despair of a Ghalib or the irrepressible romanticism of a Meer, and many others in Hindi later. I just hope this does not become too confusing or clumsy a burden for poetry or for me. You have so much to choose from. I chose from a vast and ever-expanding repertoire of world poetry and learnt hopefully a lot about what poetry in our times can attempt to do. And yet under so many influences you have to carve out your own voice and in the more self-assuring moments, I would claim that such a voice I have been able to evolve, for good or bad. But I am not sure.

RJ: But this voice is in Hindi and India is a country of diverse languages. How do you establish contact with diverse languages and religions of India?

AV: Again there are many ways of looking at it. After all important poets in India in the modern period, from Rabindranath to our times, important poets have become known, accepted, read in translation in many other Indian languages. I have been translated into many Indian languages, I have books in Marathi, Gujrati, Bengali, Urdu, Oriya, Rajasthani, etc. That is one aspect. Secondly, there is a lot of give and take among these languages. Multilinguality is a fact but porousness of languages is also a fact. Thirdly, every Indian poet, although he may or she may choose to write in a single language, knows three or four languages. That's almost the norm. You would know the neighbourly languages. For instance I know English, I know Urdu, I know Sanskrit,

Talking Poetry. Ramin Jahanbegloo, Oxford University Press. © Ramin Jahanbegloo 2022.
DOI: 10.1093/oso/9780192869180.003.0028

but I write in Hindi. One can best write in one's mother tongue. And the disadvantages of writing in the mother tongue in a globalized world are there. But also the same globalized world affords opportunities, of transnational reception. I have this book 'Mandalas of Words' by a Polish scholar looking at a Hindi poet translating her work into English and getting it published in Berlin! There are as many as four countries involved in it, in a manner of speaking.

28

The Poetic Impetus

RJ: Do you consider yourself the poet of all Indians?

AV: It would be too preposterous to make such a claim. I am a Hindi poet and by the same token, I am an Indian poet and by the same token, I am an international poet. One makes me inevitably another. I would not have reached this internationality without being a poet in Hindi. I have books in French, German, Polish, English translation. When I go to international readings and poetry festivals and anybody who reacts, and not everybody reacts, but whoever does react, comes and says that there was something distinctly coming from India. I don't know myself what is that because I am not only being an Indian, I am making an attempt to be a poet to be from wherever. It is evident that the mother soil and the wind of India stick to the poetic expression and others are able to see it, whereas you may not even be aware of it.

RJ: I think you have tried to follow the Tagorean way of synthesis between the East and West without necessarily becoming a blind imitator of the West.

AV: I would say not only me but there are many Indian poets who have followed this path, without claiming to do so. All important poets in India have translated other poets, from other Indian languages, but in this context, more importantly from many international languages. Many of them have translated, through English, Western poetry, poetry of the Middle East, Asia, Latin America, Africa, China, Japan, etc. I can't think of an important poet who has not done this translation, there is an almost compulsive urge to translate. But you cannot get prestige in India through translation, unfortunately, and you hardly get any money. But still many have done it out of love, out of a desire to see how poetry of the world looks and sounds in their mother tongue. And this has been happening, much before the so-called globalization. It has nothing to do with globalization. It was trying to

Talking Poetry. Ramin Jahanbegloo, Oxford University Press. © Ramin Jahanbegloo 2022.
DOI: 10.1093/oso/9780192869180.003.0029

be part of the world on your own terms. If you want the world to receive you, you have to receive the world in your own home. And this kind of gesture has been on.

RJ: But such an intercultural effort is more apparent in a poet like you in comparison to a contemporary poet like Kailash Vajpeyi.

AV: Well there is a difference of temperament and all that. In fact it was Kailash Vajpeyi who was abroad, not me. He was in Mexico and elsewhere for some years teaching and also some diplomatic assignments. (RJ: But he didn't write poetry in English) But I did not write in English either. I don't write in English, poetry, I write critical works, that too largely about Hindustani music, visual arts, and sometimes about culture. But I am not a writer in English, and Kailash Vajpayee was not. I have pursued the path of trying to locate contemporary poetic effort of India in the world context, let's say more than Kailash did. More than maybe some other more talented people have done. Also because of circumstances.

RJ: One should not forget that you are also a cultural manager and an animator of ideas. You make an effort to be present in the Indian public space. How do you define this impetus? What gets you going?

AV: Well the impetus, I had never thought of it in this way, as you mention it. Let me put it this way, I don't know how to put it in any other way— One, from my very early days in poetic career I started imagining that we should have a place in the world in poetry, because, after Rabindranath, no modern Indian occupied any space, nobody had made that attempt either. Not for oneself but for a broader body of Indian poetry and poets. So somehow that got into my head. So when I was an undergraduate, I translated a Dutch poet; in a Hindi poem of mine I used as an epigram one line from a Portuguese poet. Things of that kind. So it was somewhere in my mind. Then some opportunities came by and partly you have to create these opportunities. It has been kind of an unannounced quiet project of bringing world attention to contemporary Indian poetry and also vice versa. I organized an Asian Poetry festival in Bhopal in 1988 and a World Poetry Festival in Bhopal in 1989 to which poets as different as Ernesto Cardenal from Nicaragua to Jurrarz from Argentina to Tomas Tranströmer from Sweden, a poet who got the Nobel, Nicanor Parra, Stephen Spender, Miroslav Holub these were very different poets. So as you mentioned

I animate and things like that, I have always thought of my role, for good or bad, that I am not just born to be a poet, I am also born to take up the cause of poetry and many other things. While being, hopefully, a reasonably good poet, I felt it was not enough. For me it also became necessary that I create fora and opportunity, occasions, and facilities for translation, for meeting people. Even at the level of India itself, I do a lot of it. In September, we have something like 40 Hindi poets and critics coming together in Jaipur for a 3-days. In November we have more than 50 poets and critics in Hindi, coming together in Raipur. In November we have 60 young Hindi writers, both fiction and poetry coming together for 3 days. So it's an ongoing thing. I nearly succeeded in having Bihar government fund a World Poetry festival on Satyagraha, which I was calling 'Truth of Poetry in the Post-truth Times'. But that has fallen through because the Chief Minister changed his political affiliations.

29

The Solidarity of Empathy

RJ: So for you poetry is also a form of education?

AV: Yes, I think poetry is, if you are vulnerable to it, make you see a little more, hear a little more, see a little more, love a little more, reject a little more, protest a little more! It accentuates, enhances, deepens. And finally it teaches you how to feel the other. The other could be nature or God or whatever, objects. It creates a bond, a kind of a human, shall we say, family, a solidarity of empathy where there are not only other humans, but there are leaves and birds, and this that and the other, ideas, so it's a family.

RJ: What role has secularism, as a mode of being, played for you in your effort to present Indian poetry and Indian poets to the world?

AV: It has been extremely important to me, I am a non-believer and yet I believe in the spiritual and I think the way the political implicated the secular in it has been very unfortunate. Even the poets, who had had the gift of belief, have written poetry which was not exactly in keeping with their religious beliefs. There is a long tradition of that in India. They have deviated from their own religious belief, iconography, and subverted that belief going in a different poetic direction in distinct ways. In tradition itself, the dichotomy between the religious and the secular does not exist so sharply as it came to exist in our modern times. I think the secular is not meant to deny the role of the sacred or the role of the spiritual, your relationship with your father/mother is a sacred relationship, there is nothing religious about it, but it is sacred, it is inviolable. And I think that a great or an important poet can only be secular without closing oneself to feel of the divine or apprehension of the sacred or intensity of the sensuous. But in our times religion has been replaced by ideology. The ones who matter are the ones who transcend it, subvert it. There would be very few important poets that could be created by religion itself or by ideology. They assume

Talking Poetry. Ramin Jahanbegloo, Oxford University Press. © Ramin Jahanbegloo 2022.
DOI: 10.1093/oso/9780192869180.003.0030

significance only by exceeding religion, by subverting religion, by superseding religion, and similarly ideology. So in my notion, this is not the same secular as is commonly understood in its political meanings which are so unfortunate and, often, unwarranted.

RJ: And where does the process of taming of violence, come in? I think poets tame the violence of the world with their words.

AV: Well again, violence partly there has been, shall we say, poetry that has supported violence, there has been poetry in Indian tradition that has supported war and is written in praise of courage, valour, and fighting spirit. Nationalism, in a militant nationalism form, is a much later phenomenon. Even earlier we had the 'veer gathas' (Chronicles of the brave) which were chronicles of valour, fighting of great wars, etc. There has been a tradition of such eulogizing of war, bravery, etc. and I think starting from the Mahabharatha itself in the Indian context, poetry has also been anti-war and anti-violence. Even when it is being written about violence, its final implication or resonance is anti-violence. It believes in the vanity and vacuity of war and violence. It enacts out the absurdity and the aridness of violence in many different ways. It may not say that directly, although there are many examples where it may do so depending on the occasion, when you think of poetry, you think of love, nature, death, immanence etc. You do not think of violence. Two of the most violent happenings of the 20th century—the Soviet empire and the Nazi empire, they both produced great poets but all dissidents. None of them ever supported violence, even though, Stalin after all fought a great war and won it against the Nazis. But Russian poetry, significant Russian poetry is of the dissidents Marina Tsvetaeva and Akhmatova, Osip Mandalstam, and Mykovsky. In other countries which were under Soviet empire, similar major poets were all dissidents. The Nazis did not produce a single outstanding poet. I mean poets might have fallen into the trap but I cannot remember any poet who became important for his Nazi beliefs. Hatred and violence are inherently antipoetic.

RJ: Poets also can fall in the trap of ideology. We have two good examples in French poetry: Paul Eluard and Louis Aragon. There is a famous poem of Eluard where he says that if the Communist party didn't exist he would have committed suicide. I wonder what happens in the mind of such a great romantic poet to write a poem like this?

AV: Well the point is that everything cannot be explained logically. Poets like any other category of people are vulnerable, especially those who are romantics in some sense, who have an imagination which can be termed as romantic, are prone to falling into this trap. Because for whatever reasons, and the reasons are probably not all that simple, they are complex, fall into the trap, and see the communist reality or the Soviet reality as a romantic dream coming true. You want a society which is without exploitation, where class distinctions have been demolished, these are very romantic ideas. I mean Marx was a great romantic, it must be said to his credit. And he created a romanticism that lasted for so long. Like Satre never spoke against the homicide that was being perpetrated by Stalin. Poets are not infallible in other words. But we should also take into account certain other aspects. Neruda wrote a poem in praise of Stalin but that does not demolish his great love poetry (Cantos). Similarly about Paul Eluard, his romantic poetry is absolutely first rate and that remains, despite of political errors that he might have committed. Yeats is a great poet, in spite of his woolly politics. Rilke was sort of thinking at that time that perhaps this is a new era coming! So they have been not exactly infallible which proves that they are only human, and that poetry is not necessarily a very dependable resistance to political stability or political romanticism or political reality.

30

The Last Man on Earth

RJ: Let us that the last human being on the planet Earth is a poet. What do you think this poet will write about in the absence of all other human beings?

AV: Well I would imagine that if the last person is left but the entire humanity has gone, such a person will be a very desperate poet in the first place. Secondly she would still imagine a new world coming up somewhere, he would still imagine that it is possible to create from nothing.

RJ: If you were reborn would you like to come back to life as a poet, or maybe you would prefer to be a musician?

AV: No no, I would still prefer to be born as a poet in hopefully much better circumstances where poetry matters and poets matter. But even if they don't I am quite willing to accept my marginality as a category of people but I would certainly like to be reborn as a poet. Because being reborn as a poet can mean the opportunity also to be a musician, a painter, within the world of words that I can fabricate.

RJ: Well, I think we can finish on this note. Thank you again for your participation in these interesting conversations.

Talking Poetry. Ramin Jahanbegloo, Oxford University Press. © Ramin Jahanbegloo 2022.
DOI: 10.1093/oso/9780192869180.003.0031

Ashok, the Poet Disguised

It is difficult to know who the real Ashok is: a poet, a writer-commentator, an administrator, a cultural activist, or is he all these rolled into one? When I first came to know him in the late 1960s, he appeared to be an enlightened bureaucrat running a literary journal and publishing booklets of poetry by known and lesser-known names from the small town of Sidhi in Madhya Pradesh where he was the district collector. I had not the faintest idea of the poet in him.

I got to know him better when he moved to Bhopal. When he was the culture secretary of Madhya Pradesh, the state had begun to support creative talents in arts and had instituted the Amrita Sher-Gil Fellowship in visual arts, the Muktibodh Fellowship in literature, and the Alauddin Khan Fellowship in Music. During the proceedings of the jury of the Sher-Gil Fellowship I asked Ashok about the criterion of selection and he said 'Nothing but excellence' and when I asked what was expected of the fellows he said 'Nothing'. He added, 'We just want them to continue working in their chosen field'. He emphasized that 'We are not doing any favour to them by giving the fellowship. We only acknowledge their excellence and offer the fellowship so that they continue to work without any encumbrance'. My impression of his being an enlightened bureaucrat was confirmed.

The city of Bhopal in the 1970s was not associated with arts and culture but this 'enlightened bureaucrat' began dreaming of turning it into a cultural hub. The idea of Bharat Bhavan took shape gradually when he began to gather support from artists like J. Swaminathan and other practitioners of performing arts and literature. He even convinced the then chief minister of the state about its feasibility and the impact it would have when the project would be realized. The state government engaged the celebrated architect Charles Correa to design the multi-arts complex for Bharat Bhavan. Correa termed his project a 'no building' in the sense

Talking Poetry. Ramin Jahanbegloo, Oxford University Press. © Ramin Jahanbegloo 2022.
DOI: 10.1093/oso/9780192869180.003.0032

that it would not be visible as a structure towering over the land but rather an eco-friendly building that merged with the environment. Built on the slope of Shamla Hills in Bhopal overlooking a vast lake, it is not visible until you reach its gate.

Bharat Bhavan was an entirely novel and creative enterprise. It was visualized as a national art centre with roots in the region yet with an international outlook. Unlike the isolated buildings of various akademis in Delhi, the Bhopal model brought together the visual, performing and literary arts under one roof. It incorporated workshops in printmaking and ceramics, closed and open auditoria, campus residencies for musicians and an archive of poetry of all Indian languages. In a nutshell, it reflected various aspects of Indian cultural practices in their diversity and multiplicity. Or, in other words, it articulated the federal construct of the Indian political system through the metaphor of art practices. In addition, it was a blueprint for such centres in all the states of India. The Madhya Pradesh government also initiated national awards in recognition of the contribution of major art practitioners.

Bharat Bhavan as a multi-arts complex was largely articulated by the partnership of Ashok and Swaminathan. It housed contemporary urban art of the country in the company of rural-tribal arts of the state of Madhya Pradesh. The adivasi art section curated by Swaminathan with his inimitable insight astounded all. Bharat Bhavan soon emerged as a favourite destination for artists and art lovers all over India while performances by major musicians and theatre personalities, festivals of Asian and world poetry and an international print biennale brought it international renown. The inauguration of Bharat Bhavan by the Prime Minister Indira Gandhi in 1982 announced the beginning of a new era for the city of Bhopal. The dream of this enlightened bureaucrat was realized in full measure.

Eventually, when his role was curtailed on account of setbacks faced by Bharat Bhavan, the absence of inspirational partners and changes in the political scenario, Ashok left Bhopal for Delhi. Here he bumped into the eminent painter S.H. Raza who had returned to India after a long sojourn in France. The painter found in Ashok a soulmate and thus began the story of the Raza Foundation. Ashok swung into action to organize cultural activities which stunned the connoisseurs of the capital. The Foundation saw for itself a mission to accomplish what the three national akademis of culture had failed to do. In addition to a spate of cultural events in various art practices it also undertook an ambitious Asian poetry symposium with translations of the readings in Hindi and English, further accompanied by a series of publications on art, literature, philosophy, and cultural studies in Hindi. It published 'Bahuvachan', a journal of arts and ideas in Hindi and 'Aroop' in English. And to pay tribute to the memory of the legendary painter after he passed away, the Foundation even organized a Raza Festival in his home town Mandla in Madhya Pradesh.

I have dwelt at length about the man with a mission to return to my initial question about Ashok the poet. The thirteen volumes of his literary oeuvre (*Ashok Vajpeyi Rachanavali*, Setu Prakashan, 2022) published recently came as a bolt from the blue. Flipping through these volumes I discovered to my great wonderment the amazing poet that he was besides being an incredible visionary. I had known him as a writer and editor of *Poorvagraha*, a path-breaking journal, read his thoughtful articles and essays in Hindi and English, heard him speak in public fora with great elan and learnt that he had returned his national award after the assassination of three great cultural activists. I was also aware that he wrote a regular column on current affairs. I was also familiar with his poetry, in fact I had found 'Vivaksha' (2006), a collection of his poems, admirably high in quality. But I had no idea that he had begun writing poetry from an early age and continued to publish his poems and translations of other poets nearly uninterrupted for over sixty years. It was also revealing that during the highly demanding days of the setting up of Bharat Bhavan right up to the running of the Raza Foundation he was most active and productive as a poet. But it is not his prolific oeuvre—although seventeen collections of poems are no small feat—what distinguishes him as a poet is the depth of his life-long love for the world of words. Words come to him astir with a restless desire of unravelling mysteries of the tangible and the intangible world in all their sensuous and magical lures but they also reveal their hidden strength to resist the assaults of a world gone mad. The poems on music, especially his 21-poem ode to Kumar Gandharva, sparkle with an uncanny empathy between the word and the *swara*. Not only do they reveal an intense urge to immerse in the spirit of the soil but they also enter unabashedly into the arena of life's darker depths, seeking the truth that only art can reveal. These poems are a testimony of his having lived through multiple lives in different shades of times.

How did he maintain such creative rigour and resilience, even a deeply-felt angst in the face of the demands his administrative responsibilities imposed upon him? How did he respond to the call of the heart while answering all that the head demanded? How did he deal with his oft-quoted phrase 'bahuri akela' ('utterly solitary') from Kabir in the midst of the tumult of activities he was engaged in?

I can venture two possible, somewhat contradictory responses. One that the magic and power the act of writing cast upon him in his early years remained throughout within his being, no matter what went around him. He guarded an inner solitude (the bahuri akela of Kabir) amidst the crowds he was surrounded by. Not necessarily as a retreat but as a point of resistance to forces that stood in the way of freedom to speak. Or conversely he decided to conceal his voice as a writer the way how Jorge Luis Borges had done while serving for long spells as a librarian. The volume he edited as India Dissents: 3000 years of Difference, Doubt and Argument (Speaking Tiger, 2017) speaks volumes about his civilizational sweep of concerns. He is made of different mettle than poets like Rimbaud who left the world in a drunken boat to dive into a river of oblivion. Ashok perhaps saw perpetual dissenters and instigators in Kabir and Ghalib who chose to sing and recite amidst people through dark and difficult times, nudging every poet to keep his/her soul awake from slumber.

The present conversation is a testament to dual intellects. Ramin Jahanbegloo is a perceptive and well-informed 'foreign' voice who is partially complicit in Ashok's quest. An indefatigable interlocutor, he comes armed with enquiries that would unnerve a lesser soul, but Ashok meets them midway with unusual candour, wit, and an innate wisdom obtained from his deep-rooted immersion in Indian culture. He sees in the wisdom of the soil a microcosm of much of life's complexities including dissent as an essential shield against every dogma, be it born of power of the state, religious conformism, or social evils. He employs art practice to unravel the meaning of historical truths and to counter the politics of hate. Rarely has life's spectrum been articulated so clearly and deeply through the practice of art as it is in this scintillating conversation.

Gulammohammed Sheikh
June 25, 2022.